THE COMPLETE BOOK
OF READY-TO-FINISH
FURNITURE

THE COMPLETE BOOK OF READY-TO-FINISH FURNITURE

Lou Oates

Prentice-Hall, Inc. Englewood Cliffs, New Jersey

Prentice-Hall International, Inc., *London*
Prentice-Hall of Australia, Pty. Ltd., *Sydney*
Prentice-Hall Canada, Inc., *Toronto*
Prentice-Hall of India Private Ltd., *New Delhi*
Prentice-Hall of Japan, Inc., *Tokyo*
Prentice-Hall of Southeast Asia Pte. Ltd., *Singapore*
Whitehall Books, Ltd., Wellington, *New Zealand*
Editora Prentice-Hall do Brasil Ltda., *Rio de Janeiro*

Library of Congress Cataloging in Publication Data

Oates, Lou.
 The complete book of ready-to-finish furniture.

 Includes index.
 1. Furniture finishing. 2. Furniture—Catalogs.
I. Title
TT199.4.02   1984   684.1'042'029473   84-6841

0-13-158239-9
0-13-158221-6 {PBK}

Printed in the United States of America

INTRODUCTION

In 1971, I FOUND myself in a dingy, poorly lit, "unpainted furniture" store. I was poking around for a low chest to fit under a window in our dining room. My wife, Barb, had been in the store the previous day but refused to go back. She felt uneasy with the dingy surroundings and the gruff man who reluctantly answered her questions. At the time, I was looking to start my own business, so my wife's bad experience roused my curiosity enough to visit the store and look around.

I saw very quickly why Barb didn't like shopping there. Pieces of furniture were stacked nearly to the ceiling. Aisles were barely wide enough to squeeze through. What little light filtered through the bare bulbs on the dirty ceiling was quickly blocked by towering piles of fur-

niture. Even I felt uneasy—and I was a veteran shopper of the local antiquated lumberyards.

"Hey," I said to myself, "I know nothing about retailing or furniture, but if I can't do better than this I deserve to stay in advertising all my life."

That store has long since gone out of business, but despite the lack of decent furniture displayed there, I distinctly remember seeing items that I had no idea were available unfinished. And the more I surveyed other ready-to-finish furniture stores, the more I realized the tremendous potential of the industry. Here was all-wood furniture at a fraction of the prices the finished furniture stores were asking.

Within a year Barb and I opened our first store and called it Naked Furniture.

Figure I-1. The unpainted furniture shop, circa 1972.

In the next ten years Naked Furniture became the largest retailer of ready-to-finish furniture in the world. This success was due not only to the abilities of ourselves and the excellent people who worked with us, but to the exciting nature of the product itself.

Most of today's ready-to-finish furniture stores are a far cry from the first one I visited. Ten years ago, no more than a few hundred items were manufactured specifically for the ready-to-finish customer. Today, there are literally thousands of different items available to

the do-it-yourselfer. But, unfortunately, no ready-to-finish store can hope to show more than a tiny fraction of that selection. And since so few stores are set up to take special orders, many of the most unusual and desirable items go undiscovered.

It's no wonder that 99 percent of the public still thinks that all it can buy in a ready-to-finish store is a plain pine chest, suitable only for hiding in the kid's room or basement.

It was this misconception of modern ready-to-finish furniture that led to the writing of this

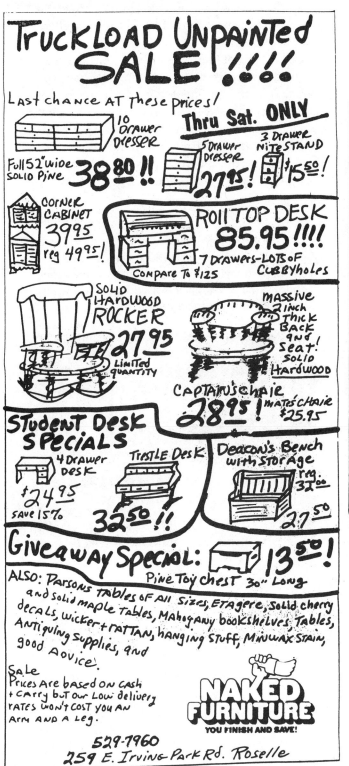

a

b

Figure I-2 a. and b. Nothing portrays the changing face of an industry as much as advertising. Here's a rustic (to put it mildly) Naked Furniture ad I prepared in 1973 as contrasted with a 1983 version made by our advertising agency. Note that the first item in both ads is the same. Today's ready-to-finish stores—like the ads—are much more inviting.

book. I guess that I finally got tired of people raising their eyebrows and looking down their noses at the mention of my line of work. At any rate, what is compiled here shows the tremendous range of furniture that is now available, where to find it, and how to properly finish it.

I've had first-hand experience with most of the manufacturers featured here. In every case, I have selected only those with whom I have dealt with personally through Naked Furniture business, through my own detective work at industry trade shows, or through recommendations of associates whom I know to be excellent judges of quality.

This is not the type of book that needs to be read from page one to the end. Perhaps you couldn't care less about how the industry got started in the sweat shops of the 1890s, but what you will find irresistible is the nearly unbelievable array of truly fine furniture you can save money on. So roll up your sleeves, pop open that can of stain, and let's get started.

Figure I-3. Finding highly styled furniture like this contemporary dining table in solid oak with parquet top is now commonplace in today's ready-to-finish stores.

Figure I-4. The avid do-it-yourselfer can now furnish entire rooms with complementary items in fine woods—a far cry from the days when only a few simple pine chests could be found.

ACKNOWLEDGMENTS

I thank the people who assisted me in the writing of this book: Linda Utterback, editor of the *Unfinished Furniture Industry* magazine; the many manufacturers who devoted considerable time and effort to this book; Pete Lehman, Ida Stein, and Neil Lang—three outstanding sales representatives who sold me my first furniture, and finally, to my wife, Barbara, without whose support this book would not have been written, and Naked Furniture would not have been born.

CONTENTS

FROM SWEAT SHOPS TO CHICKEN CRATES

So you want to know about ready-to-finish furniture! You are part of an elite minority. Right now, less than five percent of all Americans have ever ventured inside a ready-to-finish furniture store, let alone have ever purchased anything there.

For the moment let's savor the fact that you have this much-overlooked world to yourself. Why should you alert your neighbors and friends to the fact that you're going to save all kinds of money by furnishing your home with ready-to-finish furniture? Let them shell out the few bucks for this book. Let them wonder how you can furnish your home so beautifully and creatively on so few dollars.

Before we go any farther, I'd like to get something straight about the name. Is it un-painted, unfinished, or ready-to-finish furniture? I hate the term "unpainted." It's the earliest known name to describe the product—coming from a time when hardwood chairs were only 60 cents each. But to me "un-painted" means that you've got to cover up a poor-quality wood with paint. That's certainly not true today with the high-quality items available.

So the first lesson you can learn from this book is that you should purge "unpainted" from your vocabulary.

By the same token, "unfinished," while still the workhorse name of the industry, also has bad connotations. To me it means that it's not completed—which is technically true I sup-pose—but in the minds of customers it also means that it may need a lot of other work. I've had prospective customers on the telephone worrying over their lack of woodworking ability. They liked the furniture, but they believed that they must be able to saw, plane, and cut wood to properly prepare the item. So you won't find any references to "unfinished furniture" in this book.

"Ready-to-finish," on the other hand, means exactly what it says. It's ready to finish. With the exception of a few easily gained skills that you'll learn in chapter six, no specialized finishing knowledge is needed.

Most furniture comes fully assembled and cartoned. The items that do require assembly are usually manufactured with all connectors attached so that only simple household tools are needed.

What makes it even easier for the do-it-yourselfer is that today's ready-to-finish furniture is factory-sanded to a degree not possible a few years ago. You will no longer need the shoulders of a middle linebacker to withstand the rigors of hours of work with a stack of sandpaper.

Quality control is also at an all-time high, so any repair work to correct factory defects are minimized. And with the better quality stains and finishes now available, getting the attractive, durable finish you want is quite easy.

Now that we've got the basic words right, let me guess the reasons you bought this book. You probably bought this book to save money on furniture purchases. Smart move. And you probably don't think too highly of the production factory lacquer finishes that are used so often on finished furniture. I don't blame you. So now you're ready to spend some enjoyable hours working on your furniture to get the quality finish you want.

Right again? This book is also for you if you don't know much about ready-to-finish furniture and have no real knowledge of what items are available, let alone knowing how to go about things with a can of stain. If these last two paragraphs don't describe you, please do not return this book. There's always room for one more.

There's something else I know about you. You'll thoroughly enjoy your experience with this furniture. Perhaps it's because you are a wood lover to begin with. Don't try to hide it—the store salespeople can sense it.

THE LAID-BACK, NO-HYPE, DOWN-TO-EARTH, READY-TO-FINISH STORE

If you feel ill-at-ease in places like the White House or the Taj Mahal, you'll feel right at home in a ready-to-finish furniture store. You'll find no slicked-up, blue-suede-shoe types here. And no fancy-schmantzy decorators, either. Most of the salespeople, if they're worth their rubber gloves, will have an open can of stain in their hands, ready to show you how to finish—usually right there on the spot. There will be sawdust underfoot in many stores and the aromatic smell of freshly sanded oak.

But the lack of formality doesn't mean there's a lack of know-how. The people in a good ready-to-finish store know their stuff. These are wood experts who in many cases also own the store. They know what finishes work best for each use. But, more important, they can help you finish your furniture the way you want it.

In the ready-to-finish store the most noticeable absence is high-pressure selling. On a "pushy salesperson" scale of one to ten (with number one being a used car salesman, and number ten being the local Salvation Army resale shop volunteer) ready-to-finish salespeople nail down the number nine position. Nobody will jump up and follow you around the store like a puppydog, looking to make the week's commission off of you.

Nor will you find that the expectation of the salespeople is to sell you a whole houseful of furniture. In many finished furniture stores, they want to sell you the entire room of furniture—and not without some reason. It's often difficult to match a finished item bought months ago with a new one. The manufacturer may decide to drop that color finish, or he may decide to drop the matching piece you planned on adding later. But too often the reason is that the salesperson wants to make a commission off you today, rather than gamble that you'll be back later.

Ready-to-finish salespeople, however, know that they're in a high repeat business. They know that they will sell you an average of one and one-half items per visit. This is partly because you're likely to buy a replacement item—a chair to replace one that was broken; or a non-multiple purchase item—a cabinet for the stereo or a new dresser for the baby.

Because you may not finish all the furniture you need at one time is good reason for salespeople to feel confident you will return. You may want to finish a table now and come back for two chairs later, after the table project is done. For budget reasons, you might wait as long as two or three months before completing the set with two more chairs.

Luckily, you seldom have to worry about matching the color. You'll probably have stain left over from the last job. If you don't, there's plenty more stain available.

With none of the pressing reasons for buying lots of furniture at once it's no wonder that less than five percent of ready-to-finish salespeople are on a commission basis. So, if you don't feel the need to buy the whole shebang now, you'll feel right at home in a ready-to-finish furniture store.

After you've decided on your first finishing project, your involvement with the salespeople begins. Not only will you look to them for advice on selecting woods, stains, and finishes; they'll share with you valuable tips on saving time on your project. It pays to get on their good side.

The next time you're in the store you'll chat freely about the item you finished. You'll describe in loving detail how beautifully you finished it and all the friends you've shown it to. This unique situation makes for a much warmer relationship than you'll experience in other kinds of stores where there's a simple customer–clerk transaction.

Believe me, I'm not buttering you up so you will rush right into a Naked Furniture store and buy furniture, although that's not such a bad idea. But Naked Furniture stores still number only about 70 stores at the time of this printing so if you do rush right out, chances are you'll buy at one of the other 1,000 or so outlets.

THE NAKED BEGINNING?

About 40 years ago, after a particularly rough night out on the town, a furniture finisher—let's call him Joe—forgot to stain a chair and stuck it in a box that somehow got shipped out.

About a week later in Yonkers, a store owner—let's call him Murray—who also had a rough night on the town and couldn't see too well, stuck the chair out on his sales floor. That same day a shopper, who was trying to find a replacement chair that matched her dining set, saw the naked chair.

"What a marvelous idea," she thought. "With this bare chair all I need do is stain it to match the color of my set!" Later that day, the shopper's hard-working husband, after a grueling ten-hour day at the mill, came home to his wife, kids, and bare chair. Before collapsing in front of the radio, he found himself dragging the chair down to the basement, where he pried open a can of stain he used on the woodwork two years before, and thus became the world's first ready-to-finish furniture finisher.

While this fictional yet plausible scenario no doubt played many times, it's hard to verify such goings-on for something as factual as a book. And besides, it's hard to admit that an entire industry could stem from Joe and Murray sopping up a few too many at the corner bar. So let's move on to the more documented version.

The real beginnings of this industry, strangely enough, did not start with the first selling of furniture to the do-it-yourselfer. The first recorded sale was as early as 1881 when Union City Chair Company made bulk sales of unassembled and unfinished chairs to the sweat shops of the textile manufacturers in New York.

Not only were the bosses paying only pennies in wages, the employees often had to assemble their own chairs if they wanted a place to sit. It's not recorded how many of the workers also finished the chairs, but I wouldn't like to bet that many workers could find the time away from their bosses.

If you want to get technical, I suppose you could count Union City Chair Company as the first bona fide ready-to-finish manufacturer in 1881, but it was actually some 39 years later, when a man working for Union City capitalized on the ready-to-finish idea to solve an entirely different problem.

Sam Salmanson was having more than his share of problems. The year was 1920 and it was a dog year in the furniture business. The economy was in no great shakes and the manufacturers Sam represented were anxiously awaiting orders that were getting harder for Sam to write every day.

The department stores that Sam called on also had housewares departments and this set Sam to thinking. "Here I am knocking myself out trying to sell this furniture buyer more of the same old items. What would happen if I sold him a few chairs without a finish for his housewares department? I bet it would sell more paints and stains for them. If it works, every time I call on this store I could sell a few extra furniture pieces."

Boy, did it work. The department stores indeed sold extra paints, stains, and varnishes. In fact, they sold much more furniture than they thought possible. Within a few years, department stores such as Wanamaker's of New York were begging their furniture suppliers for additional items sans the finish for their housewares departments.

Sam knew a good thing when he saw it. He founded Salmanson & Baumritter Company, one of the earliest distributors of ready-to-finish chairs and tables. The company, since merged into Union City Chair Company, is still one of the largest suppliers of hardwood dining chairs. (See page 109.)

Sam's marketing brainstorm stuck. Most of the original ready-to-finish furniture manufacturers and distributors are still in business today. For example, Frank & Son began supplying Wanamaker's as early as 1925 with chests of drawers, dinette tables, and chairs. In 1927, Frank & Son came out with the first catalog to feature ready-to-finish furniture. As you can see on page 63 of chapter four, Frank & Son is still a supplier of highly styled and popular furniture.

Sam Bailey, who later founded S.J. Bailey & Sons—one of the largest manufacturers in this industry—started out building wooden shipping crates for live chickens. In the late 1920s, he began to supply ready-to-finish furniture to stores on the East Coast. As you can see on pages 32 to 36 it is the well-to-do chicken indeed who could afford Bailey furniture now.

But perhaps the most explosive event in the ready-to-finish industry occurred some 25 years after Salmanson's idea first struck pay dirt.

Early one frosty February morning in 1946, Mary Harris was unhappy. Breakfast was late and heaps of washed clothing were stacked on the bedroom floor. "Clyde Harris, if I can't find a chest of drawers for these clothes by Saturday you can start fixing your own breakfast."

Clyde Harris, along with his brothers, had just built a new box mill plant in Pendleton, Oregon and were producing wood shipping boxes for apples and berries.

"Clyde, you've got all that wood down at the mill, how about building some furniture for us?" his wife implored. Dutifully, he did just that. And when Clyde finally hauled the truckload of furniture home from the mill, Mary was overjoyed. Clyde did such a good job of building their dressers, bedstead, and a table and

UNPAINTED FURNITURE
NEWEST HOUSEFURNISHING ESSENTIAL

Frank & Son
Inc.

General Offices and Display Rooms
935 BROADWAY (corner 22nd St.,)
NEW YORK CITY

Chicago Display
AMERICAN FURNITURE MART
SPACES 1013-12
Open Fridays

Figure 1-1.

Figure 1-2. Chickens can no longer afford Bailey furniture.

chairs, that Mary urged him to build more furniture to sell to others.

The next few years proved just how good an idea Mary had. Clyde showed that he could satisfy furniture customers besides his wife, because by 1949, just three years from the pile of clothes on their bedroom floor, Harris Pine Mills had become the largest producer of ready-to-finish furniture in the world. See pages 67 to 72 for Harris furniture Mary would be happy with even today.

Figure 1-3. "Our Founder." This is what most people still think of when someone says "ready-to-finish" furniture. To date, over one-half million of these grace American homes—in basements, workshops, and kids' rooms. Naked Furniture stores alone have sold nearly ten thousand of just this one item since 1972.

THE TWIG
IN THE FOREST

EVEN THOUGH THE MOST optimistic industry leaders proclaim that the ready-to-finish furniture industry in the United States will reach the $400 million sales mark this year, it's still a mere chip off the old finished furniture block. Finished furniture sales for 1984 will probably top $20 billion. That is another way of saying that very few people know anything yet about ready-to-finish furniture.

Why should you consider it for your home? You're most apt to shop for ready-to-finish furniture because you've heard that it was cheaper. So naturally, the first thing you want to know is just how much you'll save. The answer, of course, depends. Many of the manufacturers featured in this book make ready-to-finish furniture exclusively, and so the question cannot apply except to compare similar but not identical items. You can save over 50% on some items. But on other items that are available both finished and unfinished there can be as little as a 15% difference in price.

As shown on the markup chart on the next page, the retail price difference between the two can be substantial. This does not mean that you will never find a lower price for the same item in a finished furniture store. Store markups vary widely, especially during sales. But if you don't have the time to shop every store in the county, rest assured that you will pay less in a ready-to-finish store ninety-nine times out of a hundred.

Chart One—Retail Markups of the Same Item of Furniture

	Cost of Chest	Freight*	Landed Cost	Markup**		Retail
READY-TO-FINISH dealer	$ 90	10	100	×	2.0	$200
Finished dealer	100	12	112	×	2.1	235.20
Retail price difference =	$ 35.20 (a 15% savings)					

Chart Two—Retail Prices for Similar But Not Identical Items

	Cost of Chest	Freight*	Landed Cost	Markup**		Retail
READY-TO-FINISH dealer	$ 50	10	60	×	2.0	$120
Finished dealer	100	12	112	×	2.1	235.20
Retail price difference =	$115.20 (a 51% savings)					

*Freight rates for unfinished goods generally are less than those for finished furniture.

**Finished furniture dealers must add extra margin for a higher rate of returned items, higher costs of store occupancy, in-store furniture touch-up costs, free delivery in some cases, and greater number of markdowns due to outdated stock, scratched finishes, and so forth.

Without belaboring the point of the obvious price advantage anymore, let's look at some of the other differences.

WOOD QUALITY—WHAT YOU SEE IS WHAT YOU GET

When furniture is to be finished before leaving the plant, wood selection is a relatively simple job. Factory finishes are highly tolerant to differences in wood colors and grain patterns. Many factory finishes are so opaque that not only the defects—but the beautiful grain patterns as well are hidden.

This allows the manufacturer to use less-perfect cuts of the same wood. And it lets him mix woods as well. Because much of the grain is hidden by the stain and finish, he can use a mixture of, say, oak and elm for the chair backs and spindles. And for the seat, he can use a third or fourth wood—even pine.

It's a different story entirely with ready-to-finish. Because you, as the final user, will be inspecting the item before a finish is applied, the manufacturer must be extremely critical in choosing his woods. Every small imperfection will show. Even nonstructural flaws such as mineral streaks and small knots must be edited out of the final product.

If the ready-to-finish furniture maker wants to mix woods, he must choose them carefully so that the customer won't get widely different colors and grain patterns on the same piece of furniture. What the ready-to-finish customer takes home is furniture with wood as perfect as possible. You know you're getting what you pay for, with no surprises.

On the other hand, you must be realistic. Wood is wood—with all the natural variations that go with it. If you expect absolute uniformity in each and every piece, you'd be best advised to stick to the plastic laminates found elsewhere.

No Plastic, Please!

Another very obvious advantage of ready-to-finish is that it's a wood product. Today it's difficult to shop for wood furniture in the finished furniture stores. The majority of table tops, for instance, are plastic, even in many higher priced stores. Bedroom furniture features plastic tops and molded drawer fronts, especially in children's furniture.

The tradition of solid wood and all-wood furniture in ready-to-finish stores is a carryover from earlier years when all furniture was wood. But as the finished furniture industry progressed into different methods of construction with synthetics such as Formica, molded plastics, and particleboard, the ready-to-finish industry was left with a dilemma—how do you ask a customer to finish a piece of plastic? To the relief of us wood lovers, nobody came up with a good answer. In fact, attempts to use plastic of any sort on table tops or drawer fronts have failed miserably in the ready-to-finish stores. Chalk one up for the wood lovers.

In the last few years, another variation in the construction of ready-to-finish furniture has developed. Whereas ten years ago nearly all the furniture in a ready-to-finish store was solid wood, today a wide selection of veneer products are available. Five years ago, fine wood veneers over a plywood base began making inroads in the specialty shops. Many "purist" store owners took great exception to selling a non-solid wood product. But most customers soon recognized the price advantages and gladly accepted the "upstart" veneer furniture for the value that it is.

Today, a large number of furniture items are available with fine wood veneers over a particleboard core. Customers are accepting this as a way to enjoy real wood beauty at the lowest possible price.

Pride—"I Did This Buffet!"

If you get job satisfaction from replacing a light bulb, think of the intense pride in finishing a large buffet and hutch for your dining room.

Every day hundreds of weekend project experts tackle such finishing jobs with no previous experience and they do beautiful work. Very often, the first thing guests are shown is their host's latest furniture finishing project.

It's not unusual to have customers finish nearly all the furniture in their home. In our house, for example, we have some 75 furniture items that my wife and I (mostly my wife) finished.

Creativity

Besides personal satisfaction, ready-to-finish offers the homemaker unlimited decorating possibilities. Do you want a pink chair with green legs? You've got it. Do you want a jet black desk? A customer who happened to be an undertaker did—and he got it. I once sold a lady a huge cannonball queen-size bed priced at $1300. This woman was very socially conscious—she was quick to point out that she was in the store only because she wanted a bright Chinese Red bed and she couldn't find one in the regular furniture stores. While this is a little more bizarre than most, it is by no means unusual.

Decorators discovered ready-to-finish furniture stores a long time ago. Many of the highly styled furniture items you see in the national magazines began as modestly priced ready-to-finish items. One of the great skills decorators have is to take a $50 chest, add $20 worth of materials and bill the client $200. This is no put-down of decorators; it's a simple example of creativity in making a silk purse out of a sow's ear. Most ready-to-finish customers, however, prefer to make their own silk purses and cut out the middle man.

Now that we've looked at many of the things ready-to-finish furniture is, let's see what it is not.

"The Orange Crates Are Out Back, Lady"

Ready-to-finish furniture is not cheap. Despite what we've said about it being "cheaper" than a comparable finished item, you are still going to pay the price for quality furniture. You will find some very inexpensive pine or particleboard items, but you won't find a solid oak table and pay an orange crate price. You'll pay a lower price than if it were finished, yes, but you are still buying a substantial piece of furniture in a quality wood.

The prices won't bother you if you've shopped in the finished furniture stores lately. But if you haven't shopped for furniture in the last five years or so, even the ready-to-finish prices will set off "sticker shock." One day a woman complained to me very loudly that she thought my furniture was supposed to be "cheap." Even though she said she hadn't yet shopped around, she was aghast at the high prices she found in my store. She left in a huff—only to return a few days later with an apology for her remarks and an order for all the furniture for her daughter's room.

I've got to pause here to relate a shopping tip: Don't expect that this furniture will look as attractive as it would in a finished furniture store. Few ready-finish stores have attractive vignettes to show off the items. And there are no fancy colored lights to highlight the items.

To put it bluntly, unfinished wood is rather dull looking. If there isn't a large number of finished samples in the store, you may not be all that impressed with the furniture. But being the true seeker of value that you are, press on! Use your imagination to visualize a stain on that particular item. Ask to see some stain samples on the same kind of wood. Most stores will have large stained sample boards of all the major woods.

Ready-to-Finish Is Not Custom-Made

Don't expect the store to take an order for a zebrawood bookcase that's 48$\frac{1}{16}$" wide and 89$\frac{3}{16}$" tall. Ready-to-finish furniture is made on assembly lines just like other quality furniture, not in the store's back room.

Figure 2-1. The odd case of furniture inspector #12–D.

No Junk

You won't find junk in most ready-to-finish stores either. Ten years ago it was a different story. One of the first shipments of furniture into my first store was a nightmare. For some strange reason all the chests had footprints on the drawer fronts. I quickly learned why. The drawers were simply too big for the space they were supposed to fit into, so some enterprising soul at the factory had turned each chest onto its back and jumped on the drawers until they went in!

Thank God, things have changed. In the last few years manufacturers have competed vigorously and have produced the highest quality furniture in the industry's history. Even some of the finished furniture manufacturers have gotten into the act. Quality companies such as Kroehler, Athol Table, Richardson,

S. Bent & Brothers, and Ellsworth have made large inroads into the business.

Look at chapter four in this book. Every item pictured has been produced for the do-it-yourselfer, and has proved to be a successful product.

No Royalty

While you won't find junk anymore, you won't find the Hope Diamond either. If you're looking for a $5,000 rolltop desk or a Louis XIV walnut and ebony parquet dressing table, you'll just have to look elsewhere. It's also true that you won't find much walnut or mahogany. And you can forget about ebony, teak, rosewood, pecan, ironwood, and so on. So if your tastes run to the exotic woods you're out of luck. You'll find a wide range of prices and styles in a ready-to-finish store, but the extremes are found somewhere else.

HOW TO SHOP FOR READY-TO-FINISH FURNITURE

3

WOODS YOU'D LOVE TO TAKE HOME TO MOTHER

QUICK—NAME A HARDWOOD! I'll bet that the first wood that popped into your mind was oak. If not, the odds are that you thought of maple. Besides being the two most mentioned hardwoods, both are used in ready-to-finish furniture. But by far, oak is the king of the hardwoods when it comes to both customer preference and amount of furniture available in the ready-to-finish stores.

In fact, oak is also the most popular wood of the finished furniture industry—used in over 25 percent of all bedroom and dining suites.

The availability of oak for the ready-to-finish market, however, is a fairly recent development. As late as 1976, very little ready-to-

finish oak furniture was available outside of the West Coast states. The majority of furniture elsewhere was made of pine, with the limited availability of aspen, alder, and ash hardwoods. Manufacturers such as Precision Craft in Illinois and Richardson in Wisconsin were just beginning to move into ready-to-finish oak in a big way.

Since the beginning of the 80s, many other manufacturers in California and most other states have discovered the consumer demand for oak is too lucrative to pass up. The result is a startling assortment of fine oak furniture. If you live in the West Coast states you'll find solid oak furniture of a quality normally found in only the highest priced finished furniture stores. In other states, you'll have to hunt around a bit to find the very finest solid oak furniture. But excellent items do exist if you know what to look for. Many of the items shown in this book can be specially ordered by a retail store near you. Special hints are given later in this chapter to show you how to get those items at the best possible price.

If I seem to be putting oak on some kind of pedestal, it's only because oak is much easier to sell than any other wood. Customers automatically think that if it's oak, it has to be good. This may be true in most cases but it's no guarantee. In fact, many pine items made by S.J. Bailey & Sons are better built than similar oak furniture I've seen. So it will pay you to suspend judgment on woods for awhile as you learn something about the other woods available.

I've divided the woods into two groups. Major woods and minor woods. This doesn't mean that one group is "better" than the other, but simply that there's more ready-to-finish furniture made of the major woods than the minor ones.

Major Woods

Oak Very hard. Excellent for all furniture. Withstands dents and misuse. Very open grain. Attractive grain figures. Looks great in natural state or with any stain. By far now the most popular wood. Grey brown to reddish brown in color. One of the heaviest woods.

Alder Lighter weight than oak. Finer grain. Often looks brownish when unfinished. Medium hard and strong. Finishes well, especially with the medium to dark stains. One of the most widely used woods in the ready-to-finish industry (see Harris).

Pine Most-used species are eastern white pine by the eastern manufacturers such as S.J. Bailey and Ponderosa pine by Harris. Softer than most hardwoods. Distinctive grain patterns, especially with knotty varieties. Good for most furniture except chairs. Attains unique "mellowness" with age.

Minor Woods

Maple Very hard and heavy. Creamy white in color with fine, smooth, straight grain. Excellent wood for tables (see Athol Co.). One of the easier woods to finish.

Aspen Used extensively in case pieces such as chests, dressers, desks (see Khoury Co.). White color with less distinct grain than most. Softer than most other hardwoods.

Beech Very popular for chairs. Heavy, hard, and fine grain. Easy to finish well with any color stain.

Cherry, Ash, Birch Very limited use in ready-to-finish furniture. Cherry, in light to reddish brown in color (see Ellsworth), is used mainly in occasional tables. It's best stained with light colors or left natural. Ash, in gray to reddish-brown color, is used mostly as chair parts, especially in steam bent backs. (See Athol for distinctive ash case pieces.) Birch, in creamy white to reddish brown, has small wood pores and is used mostly in tables and case pieces.

WHAT TO LOOK FOR WHEN SHOPPING

Let's cover some of the construction features that make for a well-built item. Again, these guidelines only apply to ready-to-finish furniture. This is what is available to choose from— what you'll find in any ready-to-finish store.

Drawers

Drawers are the workhorses of furniture. They take as much battering as chairs and table tops. So it will pay you to make sure the drawers will do the job for which they are intended.

Do you have a choice of drawers with a given furniture piece? No. Then why go through this exercise? Simple. You may have to buy a different, perhaps more expensive, piece if you want to be picky about your drawers. And besides, knowing something about drawers will give you a good clue as to the quality of the item of furniture itself.

There are all kinds of drawers out there. Some are better built than others, but in most part, all drawers that I've had experiences with in ready-to-finish furniture are serviceable for the use intended. Here are some of the kinds you'll see:

A Good Drawer (Figure 3–1)   This is the simple box drawer, simply nailed or stapled together with or without glue. A groove is cut around the bottom to accommodate a Masonite-type drawer bottom. This is often found in the least expensive particleboard and pine furniture (see Harris). This drawer is sturdy enough for most clothing storage. For heavier storage, such as for tools in a workshop or for toy storage for an active child, I'd recommend laying an extra sheet of plywood in the drawer and gluing the drawer joints with a white glue (such as Elmer's).

A Better Drawer (Figure 3–2)   This drawer features French dovetail joints holding the sides onto the front and back. Glue is used also with most drawers of this type. The bottom is likely to be made of luan mahogany plywood or a thick masonite. Occasionally, a birch or maple plywood bottom is used. This drawer is used on most mid-priced items and will last longer than the simple box design.

The Best Drawer (Figure 3–3)   Whenever you pick up this drawer you know you have a quality product. It has a solid wood front and back, even though the sides may be plywood. There is full dovetailing in all four corners, with either a solid wood or thick plywood bottom. I've seen dovetailing like this on the corners of ancient Egyptian wooden burial vaults, so you can count on them holding up until, say, the year 6084.

Besides the "best" drawer construction itself, the furniture piece will have dust panels

Figure 3-1. A good drawer. You can strengthen it if needed.

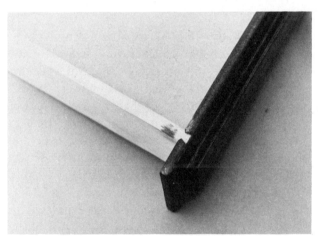

Figure 3-2. A better drawer. One you don't have to worry about.

Figure 3-3. The best drawer. One you can show off to your friends.

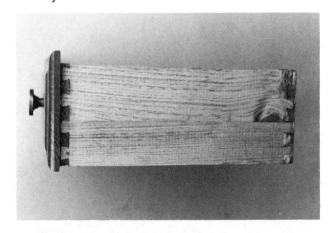

below where the drawer slides in. This is to prevent dust from settling on the contents of the drawer below when the drawer is opened and closed.

Keep in mind an interesting advantage of ready-to-finish furniture. Most of the furniture will be stocked by your dealer for a long time. If a drawer proves to be a problem, even after a year or so of use, most retailers will provide a replacement at no cost or at a small cost. Manufacturers have been generous in supporting customers through the specialty stores.

DRAWER SUPPORTS AND GLIDES

While drawers are an important consideration of the furniture you're buying, how easy the drawer pulls in and out is of equal concern. The simple fact is that some drawers "work" much better than others because of the drawer mechanism that operates it. The first thing to do to inspect a drawer is to turn it over and look underneath. The least expensive drawer will have nothing under it. It merely slides into its space rather loosely.

The "better" drawer will have a plastic or wood "center guide" installed on the rear of the drawer bottom to guide the drawer along a wood track (Figure 3–4). This is to keep the drawer centered in its space and to allow a fully loaded drawer to move easily in and out.

Furniture of this quality will also have small plastic tabs on the inside edges of the drawer spaces that serve to lessen the friction of the drawer with the drawer frame. These tabs are installed at the factory but are not always positioned correctly. Ready-to-finish stores are notorious for not always fixing this on floor samples. So if a floor sample drawer seems not to work well, don't worry. It's easily fixed by aligning the tabs—a simple adjustment. Most of the furniture in ready-to-finish stores will feature this drawer or similar types.

The "best" drawer will feature wood-on-wood center guides with a special device on the back of the drawer to prevent the drawer from pulling out unintentionally. This drawer will also be completely factory-sanded for greatest smoothness. It should be ready for finishing with very little preparation.

In the last few years, many of the contemporary-styled items have featured drawers with steel rails on the sides and roller bearings (Figure 3–5). These work very well and should be considered as desirable as the "best" wood-on-wood guides above.

THE SOLID WOOD STORY— ALL ABOUT TOPS AND SIDES

For these parts, you'll find solid wood, wood veneer over plywood, and wood veneer over particleboard. Some manufacturers are purists.

Figure 3-4. A drawer properly "center-guided."

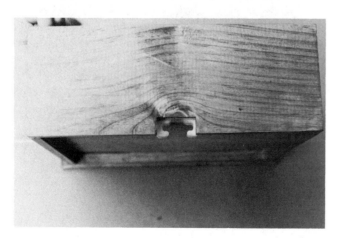

Figure 3-5. Many contemporary drawers have steel rails and roller bearings.

They would never make furniture except out of solid this or solid that. Many of our customers feel the same way. In the last few years, however, more and more manufacturers have been using veneers. For the most part, they use common sense when using veneers in order to give the maximum strength and beauty for the fewest dollars. In this book, roughly half of the manufacturers featured use veneers extensively.

The main benefits of solid wood are its strength and repairability. Wood veneers, on the other hand, are more susceptible to damage. Drop something heavy on veneer and you may be looking for the nearest furniture repairman. You must also be sure to sand veneers carefully to prevent "sand-throughs" (sanding through the veneer). Yet, when finished wisely, the veneered items look every bit as attractive as the solid ones, and often cost a great deal less. You'll be able to compare solid and veneer prices for similar items in this book.

Veneer furniture—due to its particleboard or fiberboard core—tends to be heavier, weighing as much as five times more than solid wood items. Veneers with a plywood core combine light weight with strength and are used by several top manufacturers (see Precision Craft).

I've always recommended solid wood table tops to my customers because of the ease of refinishing and repair. For the tops of, say, chests and dressers, the veneer products are fine. In fact, I'm constantly fooled into thinking an item has a solid top when, in fact, it's a very clever veneer job.

If there's any doubt in your mind if an item has particleboard in it or not, give it the quick "heft test." Grab it and lift. If it's heavier than it looks, it has particleboard in it.

Joints to Look For

If you see a joint, that's bad. Joints should be tight and designed so that the eye is attracted to other design features of the piece. Let your eyes be the judge of quality. If you're looking at a bookcase and the back is bowed away from the shelves, that tells you that you may have some trouble with durability. Look carefully at the way the tops of a chest or dresser meet the sides. If there is a noticeable gap, that item was not manufactured correctly and is out of alignment, or, it could warn you of freight damage that wasn't obvious enough to be caught by the store. There is no reason for you to accept gaps in joints. Keep in mind, however, that some joints will become much less noticeable when stained. If the floor sample shows a glaring defect but otherwise the item is what you want, ask to see another one from the store's back room or warehouse.

If you think an item is less durable than you may need, don't be shy. Grab it and shake it a little. This happens all the time in a ready-to-finish store. Customers are so tired of seeing so much vinyl junk in some finished furniture stores that they like to grab hold of some solid furniture for a change. Unless you really abuse the privilege, you will be considered a wise shopper.

HOW TO BUY A CHAIR

I am not a chair expert in the sense that I know all the detailed mechanics involved in building one, but I've helped thousands of customers choose chairs for their homes. The following sections describe the main features you'll need to know about when selecting chairs.

How to Judge a Chair

You'll probably go about this the right way naturally. First, you'll look for the right *style*. Then you'll sit in it to see if it's *comfortable* for you. Then you'll look at the *price* to see if it's what you wanted to spend.

Dining chair prices will vary tremendously in our stores, ranging from around $30 to over $200. This is more of a price range than you'll see in most finished furniture stores, so I'd like to point out some of the chair features that will justify the difference in cost.

As a general rule, the higher priced chairs will be in oak, ash, or maple, have more premium features, and be much heavier in weight. Many of the excellent quality imports are made of European beech wood, a smooth grained hardwood that is attractive, extremely durable, and easy to finish (see Hardwood Imports in chapter four). While there are some manufacturers offering seemingly well-built chairs out of pine, I have never recommended that anyone buy a pine chair except for the lightest of uses.

Features to Look For

Williams Joints (Figure 3–6) When ordinary holes are drilled at an angle, they leave an unsightly gap (A) at the joint. A Williams joint has a countersunk hole (B) that makes a snug fitting, stronger joint (C).

Leg Pins Turn the chair over. Look for countersunk holes into the main joints with screws or dowels used as reinforcements. Neat,

well-drilled holes are a mark of quality. Lesser-made chairs will have steel pins machine-driven into the main support joints. If you see none of the former qualities, you may want to choose another chair.

Rigidity Chairs must be rigid. Grab the chair by the arms or the back, press down hard and twist. The chair may *flex* somewhat—especially if it has long posts. That's okay. But any *looseness* in any joint is a danger signal—do not buy that chair.

Seat Slope (Figure 3–7) Look to see how the chair seat slopes from front to back. The better chair will distribute your weight evenly over buttocks and backs of upper legs. Sit in a lower-priced chair for one full minute and then in a higher-priced chair and you should feel this difference immediately.

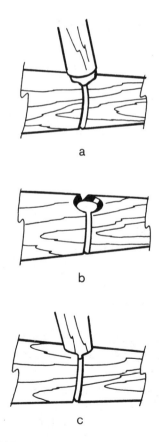

a

b

c

Figure 3-6. The Williams joint.

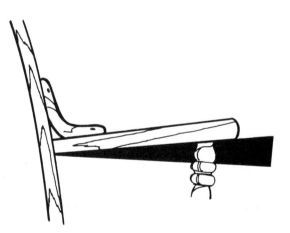

Figure 3-7. In general, the greater the angle, the more comfortable the chair.

Back Angle (Figure 3–8) The "tilt" of the back and the "roundness" of the back are both important features for comfort. These require more expensive techniques on the part of the chair maker. The better ladderback chairs, for example, have gracefully curved backs that are

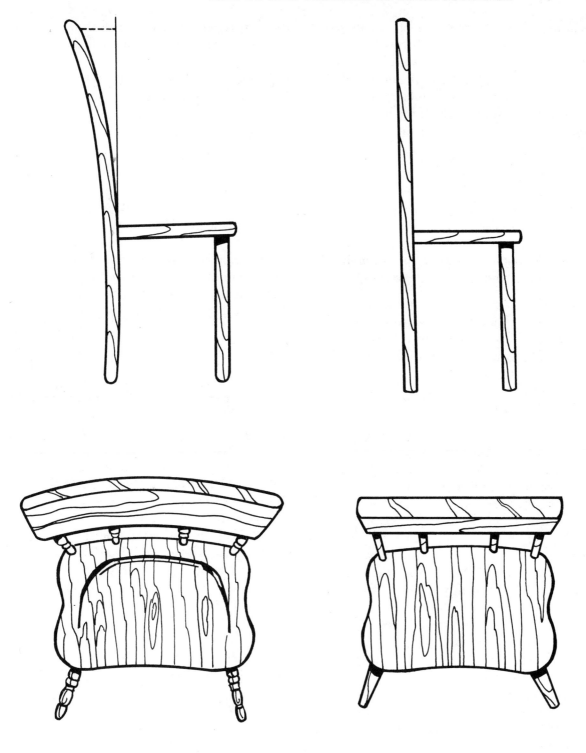

Figure 3-8. Comfortable chair has ample slant of back, curved back to cradle your back, and form-fitting seat depression called "saddling." Beware the chair on the right.

steam bent from a single piece of ash. In general, the more the back tilts back and cradles the natural shape of your back, the more expensive the chair. The back tilt can present a durability problem for some chairs, however. The long posts on the backs of the better chairs should go completely through the seat and be held securely from the bottom with a wood wedge.

Overall Trim   All the edges on the best chairs will be "feathered" so that you feel only smooth, gentle edges. The seats will be deeply "saddled." This chair will be sanded to such a degree of smoothness, you can run your hand over every part and not feel any rough spots.

Comfort   As an almost universal rule, the higher priced chairs will be more comfortable. They are a salesperson's delight. The surest way for you to buy the most expensive chair in the store is to sit in it.

How to Sit in a Chair

I don't mean to insult anyone by discussing so basic an activity, but you'd be surprised at how many customers will try out a chair the wrong way. I've had customers tell me that all the chairs in the store were too small for them. Only when I pointed out that perhaps they should take off their bulky winter coats before trying the chairs did they find the right one.

The first step is to duplicate the way you plan to use the chair in your home. Sit in the chair under the same conditions. A dining chair may seem uncomfortable unless seated at a table, so pull it up next to a table in the store as if you were eating. Many of the inexpensive ladderback chairs are fine for eating at the table, but not so fine for just sitting around.

If you are choosing chairs for a dining table you already have at home, make sure you measure how high your table is from the floor. Your table may be 28 inches high, or it may be 30 inches high. Most chairs in ready-to-finish stores are standardized at about 18 inches, so those two inches in table height can add up to a big difference in comfort. When in doubt, ask

the store to let you bring one chair home to try it. This happens often, so don't be bashful.

WHERE TO SHOP FOR READY-TO-FINISH FURNITURE

Catalogs

Most of the major department stores carry ready-to-finish furniture. Although the selection is very limited, do-it-yourselfers in rural areas may find these the only sources.

Montgomery Ward leads the list with six pages of ready-to-finish furniture made by Harris, Union City Chair Company, and others. Sears features five pages with most of the furniture supplied by Kroehler, Union City, and S.J. Bailey. J.C. Penney's selection is only four pages with items from Harris, American Forest, and others.

The prices in these catalogs are fairly competitive with the ready-to-finish specialty stores, but you must be very careful about the freight charges. Make sure you have the catalog desk quote you the shipping costs before you order. Freight charges can easily add up to half the cost of the item itself. Another possible drawback to buying from these catalogs is that you don't get to see the quality of the item until you open the box.

Also in this group are the specialty catalogs such as Yield House, The Bartley Collection, and Heath Craft. Most of the furniture that these companies make is available only through their catalogs. Many of these suppliers are featured in chapter four along with their addresses. These are truly specialists in selling high quality, ready-to-finish furniture by catalog, and as such have outstanding quality control as well as superior furniture-packing techniques. Most of their items are in kits, so shipping costs are low and the possibility of damage is minimized.

Lumber Yards, Home Centers, Discount Stores, and So Forth

The lumber yard in your neighborhood may have ready-to-finish furniture you've never seen. It's usually tucked into a corner where it won't interfere with the selling of boards and molding. Most lumber yard selections are limited to the inexpensive pine or particleboard lines. But it won't cost you much to give the larger lumber yards in your area a phone call. Most lumber yards get calls about ready-to-finish furniture often. If you ask, they may refer you to a yard that does carry the items.

Home centers have been more likely to carry ready-to-finish furniture lately due to their commitment to carry more upscale furnishings for the home. Home Depot in Atlanta, for example, will feature wide selections from most of the major ready-to-finish manufacturers. If you have a large home center in your area it almost certainly will have a good basic assortment.

Discount stores have gotten away from ready-to-finish furniture lately as the price points have risen considerably above the vinyl-wrapped finished furniture that have been their strong sellers. To maintain lower prices, discounters have tried selling ready-to-finish in the form of unassembled knock-down furniture such as from American Forest Products and Whittier with some success. In almost all cases, however, the selection in the large lumber yards and home centers will be much wider than in the discount stores.

In all of the above stores you must be content to buy from the items on display only. Special orders, such as would be needed on much of the furniture in this book, would be nearly impossible to arrange. Most of these stores are strictly self-service with little or no knowledge of finishing to assist you.

In some cases, with the aid of this book, you will be able to identify specific items and shop the discount stores for price comparisons.

Specialty Stores

Since 1975 the number of ready-to-finish furniture available in specialty stores has increased nearly 300 percent. Much of this business has come at the expense of the catalog houses, home centers, and discount stores that have found it increasingly difficult to compete with the growing number of specialty stores.

The average size of the ready-to-finish specialty store has risen from 3,000 square feet in 1975 to nearly 4,000 square feet today. Very few stores other than the specialty store can afford the floor space to devote exclusively to ready-to-finish furniture.

But store size is just part of the picture. The main advantage of the specialty store lies in its ability to keep abreast of the latest and best items manufacturers have to offer.

The specialty store also provides a number of services not found elsewhere. Besides stocking a wide selection of quality stains, finishes, and finishing materials, all stores will take the time to make sure the customer knows exactly all the steps to take to achieve a good finish. If the customer lacks the desire or the time to do the job, most stores will custom-finish furniture for customers at a reasonable cost.

If you think I'm biased in favor of the specialty stores, you're right. Ready-to-finish furniture is a very relaxed business that lends itself to special customer needs. For example, a couple shopping at the Naked Furniture store in Wheeling, West Virginia wondered if a cedar hope chest on display would be the right size. When the store owner invited them to try it out, they did. They brought in their 12-foot pet boa constrictor who found the chest to be the perfect size, thank you. I wonder how many discount stores would make such an invitation.

HOW TO GET THE BEST DEAL IN A READY-TO-FINISH STORE

If there's one section of this book that is bound to get me into trouble with store owners and managers, this is the one. But to be truthful, with proper negotiating you can pay somewhat less than the marked price, whether you're buying a Rolls Royce for your girlfriend or a cabinet for your stereo.

Getting the best price on a ready-to-finish item requires many of the same bargaining methods used on any other product. What knowledge I'm giving you here is ammunition. How you phrase the actual bargaining words is up to you.

To begin with, you must talk to the right person. That means the owner. If you can find out when the owner is there, you're halfway home. Most of the full- and part-time employees will not have the authority to bargain.

Many owners are guided by a "How much did I sell so far today?" attitude. If it's been a terrific morning for sales, price concessions will be harder to come by. On the other hand, if Tuesdays are the slowest day of the week—as they are in the ready-to-finish business—and if you show up near closing time, your chances of getting a better deal increase.

Now that you know what day to shop on and who to talk to, let's look at the next step. The size of your purchase is probably the most important single bargaining chip you can play. The average sale in a typical ready-to-finish store is about $130. If you want to haggle over a $30 chair, forget it. If, however, your order is over $500, you have the owner's attention. If it's over $1000, you also have the attention of the owner's wife, kids, and dog.

If the mere fact that you are about to represent the biggest sale of the week to him doesn't shake loose at least a ten percent "appreciation" discount, use the "order and wait" ploy. Tell him that it really doesn't matter when you get the furniture, and that for, say, an extra ten percent discount, you will allow him to reorder your items from the factory on a pre-sold basis. This will save him from dis-counting out of his existing stock, and allow him to batch the pre-sold order with other items he may need from that manufacturer, thus saving him freight costs.

This "order and wait" ploy is a reasonable one from the retailer's point of view and works best on large orders that really would disrupt his normal in-stock situation. For the somewhat smaller sale, though, the "floor sample" approach works well.

This approach requires that you accept a worn or dirty floor sample at a discount price. A good reduction would be 20 percent off, if the item requires a lot of sanding or a few minor repairs. It is a poor bargainer indeed who can't find some flaw, however tiny, in an unfinished piece of wood. Many times this appeal will work even on a seemingly perfect floor sample because it offers a sure quick sale to a picky customer. And anyway, that chest was getting a little yellow from sitting around.

If you can't do any good with the above suggestions, it's not yet time to grasp for straws. Since many stores do custom-finishing, say that you'll buy all that furniture at the regular price if they finish it for you at half of their normal charge. If you're looking for chairs try, "I'll buy six for the price of five." Or, "How about throwing in these finishing materials?"

If all else fails, there's one last straw to grab for. I don't know any store owner or manager who will refuse you free delivery with a sizeable order—no matter what the sign says over the cash register.

WHAT TO BUY

HOW TO USE THIS CHAPTER

Many manufacturers make several different furniture styles in many different price
ranges, so this chapter could not be organized
by style or price. It is arranged alphabetically by
manufacturer. If the furniture has to be assembled, or if it's in unassembled form requiring
special skills, I have noted it.

Throughout this chapter, I've highlighted
as many details as space or common sense

would allow. Where applicable, sizes and prices
are indicated. Keep in mind that all these de-
scriptions are approximate. For more detailed
information, see your nearest ready-to-finish
specialty store. If you can't get the necessary information there, use the Product Information
Request Forms in the back of this book to contact the manufacturer directly. The address and
phone number are listed for each manufacturer
in this chapter. Most will provide a catalog if
requested.

American Forest

American Forest is a major supplier to specialty stores, department stores, and discount stores. Prices will vary widely. You'll find these products available almost anywhere in the United States. American Forest is a large-volume producer with excellent quality control. Kits are well designed, very durable, and fairly simple for most people to put together with just a hammer and screwdriver. All hardware is included. Replacement parts are readily available directly from the manufacturer.

American Forest Products
P.O. Box 8220
Stockton, California 95208
209-946-5800

The "Encore" line is made from thick-cut Western pine. The audio tower, $79; and the entertainment "L", $119; are 16″ deep to accommodate most components. Coffee table, $59.

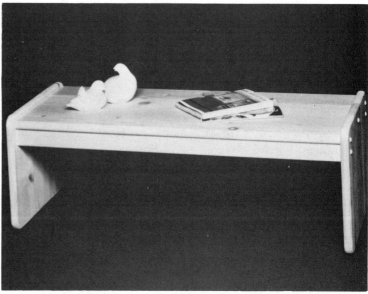

American Forest (continued)—
Unassembled Kit Furniture

"Master-Pieces" is the name of these solid pine kits. All joints are French dovetail and/or notched construction. Approximate prices: seven-drawer double dresser, $140; armoire, $160; rolltop desk, $189; four-drawer chest, $99.

Antique Creations

Solid oak dry bar with curved glass, brass rail, and rope twist turnings, about $950. Mirrored back bar, about $329.

Heavily carved and saddled 19th century bar stools in solid oak or cane and oak seats. Choice of 24″ or 30″ heights, about $179.

Antique Creations
909 C. Street
Barling, Arkansas 72923
501-452-7217

Antique Creations (continued) Country Charms—19th Century

Massive solid oak furniture with unique features. The 48″ round extension table is about $559. China cabinet with light plus spool cabinet on top, about $559. Pressback dining chairs with unique phoenix back design are about $119.

Country Kitchen

Informal 19th century style for the smaller kitchen. Authentic reproduction of china cabinet is about $295. The 36″ extension dining table is about $349. Bow back side chair, about $110. All are in solid oak.

Athens Furniture

Athens uses only first quality clear oak in all cabinets. Oak-faced plywood is used on drawer bottoms and case backs.

Athens Furniture
P.O. Box 929
Athens, Tennessee 37303
615-745-1833

Leading off an excellent selection of oak specialty items are these entryway items. Lighted console plus oval mirror, $319. Gossip bench, $189. Tea cart, $279. Large display curio $349. Lighted pie safe with pierced metal panels, $349 (opposite page). Secretary desk and hutch, $319. Cheval mirror, $219. Rolltop writing desk, $309 (all on opposite page).

Athol Table

Athol Table is a major supplier of finished tables to the nation's higher priced finished furniture stores. The consistent beauty and quality of these solid ash tables and case pieces are not found from any other manufacturer. Athol tables are now found in most major ready-to-finish specialty stores. This is a very large line. Ask the store if you can look through their catalog for additional items. You can expect to save from 30 to 40% by buying these as ready-to-finish items.

Athol Table Manufacturing Co., Inc.
Athol, Massachusetts 01331
617-249-3264

Solid ash Hadley trestle table, $549. Half china with buffet, $1047. Buffet/server alone, $557. Millers side and arm chairs, $120 and $159.

Half china with buffet, $813. Buffet/server alone, $417. All solid ash. Butterfly side table, 22″ high, $139.

Sofa-back table with two drawers, $219. Tuffet tables, $93 each. Country work table, 36″ square, $169. Dining table/desk, 34″ × 60″, $305. Country game table with sliding-top storage, $254. Tuffet tables, $93 each (opposite page).

All tables are solid ash.

S.J. Bailey & Sons

S.J. Bailey is one of the largest and oldest manufacturers in the ready-to-finish business. Items feature thick cuts of solid eastern knotty pine with firm knots and excellent white color. Woods are selected for the beautiful wood grain inherent in eastern pine lumber. Drawer joints are dovetailed with wood-on-wood center guides. Distribution is national with most outlets east of the Rocky Mountains. Pricing on this line is extremely competitive. Although they do not make these items available finished, comparable finished items are often twice the price. This is a very reliable furniture maker with a solid reputation for customer service. Another notable feature of this line is its excellent cartoning, which protects the items from possible damage before you get them home.

S.J. Bailey & Sons, Inc.
Clarks Summit, Pennsylvania 18411
717-586-1811

Large, 62″ long solid pine hutch and buffet, $619. Two-door corner cabinet is 76″ tall, $195. One-drawer washstand, $129.

Country corner cupboard, $199. Solid pine drop-leaf trestle table is 59″ × 45″ when open, $195. Solid pine 63″ seven-drawer dresser with four-drawer mirror hutch, $539. Matching armoire, $279 (opposite page).

S.J. Bailey & Sons (continued)

Solid pine 52″ wide rolltop desk, $399. Mate's bookcase desk with lift-up storage under top, $139. Cannonball bed in queen size, $259.

Solid pine Queen Anne designs. Drop-leaf cocktail table, $149. End table, $129. Sofa table, $179. Drop-leaf home sewing workshop $249 (opposite page).

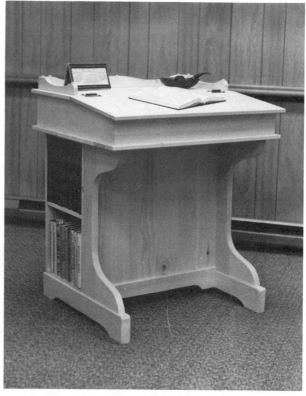

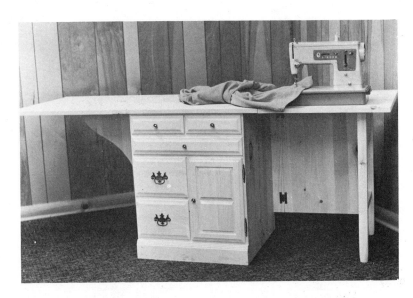

S.J. Bailey & Sons (continued)

Solid pine electronic furniture. Home computer center with top organizer, $179. Corner TV cabinet, $119. TV stand with video game cart on casters, $109.

Baker Road

Baker Road beds come knocked down for simple customer assembly. Full instructions included. Distribution is mainly in the central states. The owner of Baker Road, Tom Karkos, was the first employee I hired after founding Naked Furniture. He makes an excellent product that we're happy to feature in our stores.

Baker Road
607 Church Road
Elgin, Illinois 60120
312-695-2377

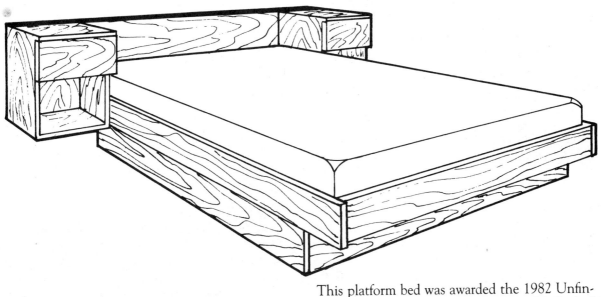

This platform bed was awarded the 1982 Unfinished Furniture Industry's Shubie Award for best design. Made of oak veneer over plywood, the platform bed includes headboard with hanging night stands. King size, $409. Queen, $389. Double, $379. Twin, $349.

Storage platform bed features solid oak drawer frames with steel and nylon drawer glides. Available with drawers on one or both sides. Prices for bed with two drawers are: king, $529; queen, $479; double, $439; twin, $379. Add about 7% for drawers on both sides.

The Bartley Collection— Kit Furniture

If your tastes run to Chippendale, Queen Anne, and other related styles, and you have the time to devote to exact reproductions in kit form, send for Bartley's catalog. This Queen Anne table is a reproduction of the table from the Decorative Arts Gallery at the Henry Ford Museum. Choose solid Honduras mahogany or Pennsylvania cherry, $425. To give you an idea of how much you'll save by finishing this table yourself, the finished cost is $970.

Chairside bachelor's chest, $195. In solid Honduras mahogany or Pennsylvania cherry. Dovetailed oak drawers.

Bartley furniture is available only through their catalog.

Bartley Collection, Ltd.
121 Schelter Road
Prairie View, Illinois 60069
312-634-9510

Bear Creek

Bear Creek is primarily a finished furniture maker, but will provide their items without the finish to specialty stores. Many of the ready-to-finish stores will carry these large oak rolltop desks finished because of the difficulty with finishing them once they are assembled. These are all premium quality items.

Bear Creek Furniture Mfg. Corp.
203 Ramsey Lane
St. Louis, Missouri 63011
314-394-9400

Traditional solid oak rolltop desk is loaded with features: raised solid oak panels; desk light; bow front cubby hole construction; hidden fire-resistant security box plus much more. Drawers feature solid oak sides and doubler roller guides. This model is 62″ wide, 29″ deep, 49″ high, $2200.

Oak executive desk is 72″ wide, 35″ deep, 30″ high. Features solid oak panels, dovetailed constructed drawers, file drawers on double roller guides and a scribes board on both right and left sides, $1200.

Solid oak legal size file cabinets are 20″ wide, 26″ deep, and 32″ or 44″ tall. Features pullout workboards and solid oak raised panels on three sides. Two-drawer, $419. Three-drawer, $509.

Bedford—Kit Furniture

Bedford specializes in furniture kits of solid cedar, cherry, walnut, and other fine woods. Their line features nearly two dozen hope chests plus cedar wardrobes, bedroom furniture, and occasional furniture of all kinds. Bedford sells mainly by mail directly to customers through their thirty-page color catalog. These are true kits, requiring you to be handy with many standard woodworking tools such as saws and clamps.

Bedford Lumber Company, Inc.
P.O. Box 65
Shelbyville, Tennessee 37160
1-800-251-1422

Computer center is 47½" wide, 20" deep, 43" high. Available in solid cedar, $119.95, in solid walnut, $159.95.

Solid cedar hope chest with solid walnut trim is 46" wide, 20" deep, 20½" high, $94.50/kit.

S. Bent & Bros.

S. Bent has become the premier chair maker for ready-to-finish stores, offering the finest quality construction, comfort, and reasonable prices. As I mentioned in chapter three, the easiest way to sell the most expensive chair in the store is to get the customer to sit in it. And with S. Bent, that goes double.

S. Bent & Bros., Inc.
85 Winter Street
Gardner, Massachusetts 01440
617-632-4300

Unique, double-embossed oak chair with solid seat features Williams joints, 1½″ thick saddled seat, and full length steam bent back posts for comfort and strength. Chair back is solid wood with very deep and detailed embossing, $139.

"Oak Hill" rocker features steam bent bannister and spindles, extra large runners, Williams joints, and deeply embossed design on steam bent back. The steam bent back on this rocker is unique—I've never had a customer who didn't say it was the most comfortable rocker they'd ever sat in. It's 47 pounds of comfort. This is one of the most popular selling large rockers in ready-to-finish furniture stores, $259.

"Douglas" chair in oak/ash construction features one-piece steam bent arm bow with steel rods through seat and stretcher, authentic beaded turnings, and deeply saddled seat, $139.

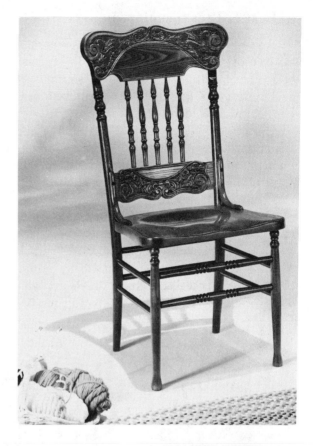

S. Bent & Bros. (continued)

"Governor Carver" chairs are made of solid birch/maple with Williams joints, steam bent backs. Arm chair has one-piece steam bent arm bow. Arm chair, $149.

"Country Tavern" chairs all feature Williams joints, steam bent backs, and solid birch/maple construction. Side chair, $79. Arm chair, $129.

Solid oak bow back chairs feature one-piece bows and back bows, wood pinned top bows, Williams joints, and deeply saddled 2″ thick seats. Side chair, $149. Arm chair, $199. Note: These bow back chairs are heavy and solid—the arm chair weighs nearly 30 pounds.

John Boos

John Boos uses strictly first quality materials in every piece of butcher block furniture they make. All wood is either solid northern hard rock maple, or solid Appalachian red oak. Impeccable workmanship is the rule with this company, which turns out heirloom quality butcher block products. Virtually every table they make—and they make dozens of different tables—is available in several sizes. Distribution is nationwide, with a natural finish. If you are looking for the best quality butcher block at reasonable prices, you'd have to look hard to do better than John Boos.

John Boos & Co.
315 S. First Street
Effingham, Illinois 62401
217-347-7701

"Virginian" collection features your choice of solid oak or solid maple butcher block tables. This table is a version of a country work table design, 48″ × 30″ × 1¾″ thick. It costs $285 in maple, $342 in oak. Traditional 60″ china and buffet is solid oak, $1319. Matching solid oak Windsor chairs, $109 each.

Traditional hutch and buffet in solid oak is 48″ wide, $1119. Eighteenth century trestle table is 60″ × 36″ × 1¾″ thick, $659 in solid maple, $779 in solid oak. Windsor chairs, $109 each.

John Boos (continued)

"Americana" drop-leaf pedestal table is 36″ round, 1½″ thick, $279 in maple, $329 in oak.

Work bar is 36″ × 24″, $134 in solid maple. Essex swivel bar stool in solid oak, $175.

Country work table with 36″ overhead pot rack, $369 in solid maple.

Deluxe cuisi cart, 36″ × 24″ × 36″ high, has drawer, knife holder, electric strip, drop leaf, plus stainless steel preparation bowl with cutting board cover, $387.

Century Reproductions

Century uses only northern red and white oak, especially selected for its color and consistent grain patterns. All case pieces have full mortise and tenon joints with glue and screws. Availability is national in ready-to-finish stores. Selected items are also found in Montgomery Ward's catalog.

Century Reproductions
P.O. Box 946, 208 N. 4th Street
Blackwell, Oklahoma 74631
405-363-3350

Solid oak claw-foot extension table features delicate carvings on apron and heavy double equalizer glides for easy opening and closing, about $659. Mirrored curio china cabinet with ball and claw feet, lighted, about $639. Double pressback chairs, $159 each.

Solid red oak cheval mirror with design pressings on top and bottom, 1/4" glass plate, $295. Stackable bookcase in solid oak. Each shelf section, $109. Top section, $59. Base section, $34.

Chattahoochee

Solid hardwood case pieces with dove-tail drawers with center guides and brass pulls. Joints are mortised and tenoned. Woods used are both poplar and cottonwood. Chattahoochee is sold mainly through specialty stores, but some home centers may carry it. Distribution is national, but concentrated in the Southeast. Representative prices are: Five-drawer chest, $149; nine-drawer dresser with mirror hutch top, $419.

Chattahoochee Furniture Co.
1 Railroad Street, P.O. Box 127
Flowery Branch, Georgia 30542
404-967-6151

Cohasset Colonials—Kit Furniture

If you can devote the time to both assembling and finishing truly authentic American Colonial furniture, send for Cohasset's catalog. Pictured here (assembly time in parentheses): bow back Windsor side chair, $129 (45 minutes); arm chair, $165 (1 hour and 15 minutes); Queen Anne drop-leaf table, $379 (2½ hours); half-round window table, $75 (45 minutes); tavern shelf, $62 (30 minutes).

Cohasset sells only through their catalog. For the large Cohasset Colonial catalog in color, send $1.00 to:

Cohasset Colonials
Cohasset, Massachusetts 02025
617-383-0110

Full size low bed, $298 (2½ hours). Canopy frame, $34 (45 minutes). School bench, $53 (30 minutes). Concord foot stool, $27 (30 minutes).

Contextural Design

This is a rather new ready-to-finish company that has grown rapidly by providing exceptionally well-designed items at practical prices. Distribution is national with concentration in southern states.

Contextural Design
6925 Old Wake Forest Road, P.O. Box 17105
Raleigh, North Carolina 27619
919-876-8461

Contemporary-style seating group available in oak with choice of many fabrics. These are very easy to assemble with clear and complete directions provided. Representative prices: arm chair, $259; sofa, $519; love seat, $395; end table, $89; cocktail table, $99.

Oak shelving unit, $240. Oak butcher block table, 30" × 42", $179. Oak arm chairs with choice of fabric, $89 each (opposite page).

Solid oak computer table, $159. 38"w × 24"d × 35"h. Also available in pine, $99. Solid oak arm chair with casters, $109. Same chair in pine, $89 (opposite page).

Rugged child's set in pine. Table and two chairs, $99 (opposite page).

Country Home Furnishings

This company makes a wide line of oak and maple tables. Many of the smaller items are available only through special orders by stocking retailers.

Country Home Furnishings
25 Wickman Drive
Gardner, Massachusetts 01440
617-632-4530

From the Beacon Hill collection, all solid oak accessory tables. Butler's cocktail table, $249. End table, $169. Sofa table with two drawers, $249.

Also from the Beacon Hill collection, drop-leaf end table with drawer, $189. Oval drop-leaf cocktail table, $249. All solid oak.

Solid oak desk, $229. Foyer table, $199. Colonial-look TV and stereo cabinet in solid oak, $289.

Creative Ideas

Solid oak bar with 2″ solid oak rail. Bar top is 1″ thick solid red oak butcher block. Optional wine and glass rack inside, $440. Solid oak computer desk with two drawers and monitor shelf is 60″ long and 26″ deep, $350.

Creative Ideas
1050 N. Anaheim Boulevard
Anaheim, California 92801
714-635-1311

Cumberland Oak

Oak parquet tables in solid oak frames. Dining table with leaf, $395. Table made with glued and screwed corner blocks underneath. Brass aligning pins used to match fit between top and extension leaf.

Solid Appalachian red and white oak is used on this 48″ round extension table. The octagonal base parts are tongue-and-grooved for maximum strength. Dual geared extension slides are used for easy opening. Table is $309 with plain legs (see insert), or $409 with carved ball and claw feet.

Solid oak tables with bronze-tinted tempered glass. Dining table, $269. Cocktail table, $119. Lamp table, $69. Easy assembly requires screwdriver. Where allen wrench is required, it is supplied.

Cumberland Oak—Norwalk Furniture Corp.
P.O. Box 2370
Cookeville, Tennessee 38501
615-432-4171

Custom American Furniture

All Custom American furniture is made of top grades of solid eastern white pine selected for its beautifully irregular grain patterns and sound red knots. All drawers are dovetailed, glue-block reinforced and have wood-on-wood center guides with nylon stops to prevent tipping.

Doors have self-closing hinges. Custom American is distributed nationally but is primarily active in the Northeast.

Custom American Furniture, Inc.
P.O. Box 1776, High Bridge Road
Botsford, Connecticut 06404
203-426-3136

Hutch and buffet, $759. Trestle extension table has 3″ thick top, $349. Dry sink with drawer, $219. Trestle bench with back is 60″ long, $159.

Night stand, $159. Queen/double bonnet-top bed, $439. Armoire (with mirror), $529. Sixty-eight inch hutch mirror and triple dresser, $789.

Custom American Furniture (continued)

Cabinet night stand, $159. Cannonball bed in queen/double, $299. Chest on chest, $479.

Sixty-inch bar, $295. Trestle desk, $279. Cabinet end table, $159.

Corner curios, $259. Open unit, $195. China cabinet with glass doors, $359. Bar/desk cabinet, $419. Two-door open-top cabinet, $295.

Dinaire

Solid oak single pedestal table opens to 41″ × 53″, $395. Unique solid oak base with elliptical shaped ½″ plate glass top, $295.

Solid oak "Viking" side chair, $99; arm chair, $123. Two unique "Quaker Road" items with heart backs: side chair, $109; and bench, $209. All are made of solid oak (opposite page).

Dinaire Corp.
601 Ohio Street
Buffalo, New York 14203
716-852-5228

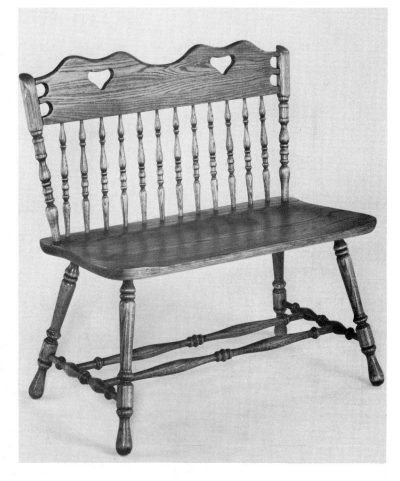

Donie Chair Company

Donie Chair has manufactured this basic line since 1903, making them one of the oldest companies featured in this book. Each item is made of solid hardwood. Primary woods are ash, hickory, and beech. The woven seats and backs are done by hand with live rush cane and natural rolled palm. These are well built, yet very inexpensive items. Adult rockers range from $30 to $70. Chairs from $22 to $40. Barstools from $19 to $50. Donie chairs are sold through major department store catalogs and specialty stores with heaviest distribution in the southern states.

Donie Chair Company, Inc.
P.O. Box 1871
Brownsville, Texas 78520
512-546-5518

Ellsworth Cabinet

Ellsworth is another example of a high quality finished furniture manufacturer that has found great acceptance by the do-it-yourselfer who appreciates working with fine wood. Northern black cherry is used in all the items pictured. Solid brass hardware is produced from antique molds. As an example of savings, the chess table pictured in this group will retail at about $339 in most fine finished furniture stores.

Ellsworth Cabinet, Inc.
4610 Hamann Parkway
Willoughby, Ohio 44094
216-951-8585

Solid cherry "Hartford" ladies' desk and bench, $569. "Brooke" tilt-top trivet table with solid brass trivet, $139.

Solid cherry "Hartford" chess table is 28″ high by 25″ square, $259. Oblong end table, $169. Oval drop-leaf cocktail table opens to 30″ × 44″, $269.

Ferguson's

Ferguson's bold country designs in solid oak are available in many southern and southeast area specialty stores, but can be ordered from dealers nationally. Select quality native oak is used along with traditional hand craftsmanship.

Ferguson's
Highway 65
St. Joe, Arkansas 72675
501-439-2234

Solid oak china cabinet with mirrored back, glass shelves, light, with eagle claw legs, $459.

Solid oak cupboard, $659. Harvest table is 36″ × 60″ with 1½″ thick solid oak top, $359. Liar's bench, $179. Arrowback arm chair, $169. Side chair, $119.

Ferguson's (continued)

Solid oak country hutch with hand-hammered copper door inserts, $1100.

Same country hutch with beveled glass, $995 (not pictured).

Solid oak butcher block extension dining table with large eagle claw legs extends to 48″ × 68″, $795. Larger 54″ × 74″ version, $849.

Solid oak country desk and clerk's registry was inspired by an old Texas farm table, $559. Continuous-arm Windsor chair, $169.

Frank & Son

Frank & Son is one of the oldest companies serving the ready-to-finish furniture industry. Their first catalog appeared in 1927. Although they still sell predominantly to east coast stores, many of their specialty items shown here are available throughout the country either as in-stock items or as easily obtainable special orders.

Frank & Son, Inc.
381 Park Avenue South
New York, New York 10016
212-889-4000

Oak hall tree with "crinkle-etched" glass mirror, $199.

Oak curio cabinet, $249.

Oak cheval mirror is 24½" wide × 56" high, with "crinkle-etched" glass, $129.

Frank & Son (continued)

Oak lighted curio cabinet with 20″ × 36″ oak-framed mirror, $289.

Oak parquet bar is 60″ wide, $289. Matching server bar is 48″ wide, $299.

Hardwood Imports

Hardwood Imports has been supplying ready-to-finish furniture specialty stores since 1980. The company prides itself on the heavy, solid European beech wood used in every chair. Beech is an exceptionally good wood for chairs, being a very hard wood with a tight grain that makes for a super-smooth finish. Beech is also very solid and heavy, much like oak. If you pick up a chair that you know isn't oak and it feels much heavier than it looks, it's probably beech. If you find yourself in a barroom brawl, this is the chair to reach for. The grain pattern of beech is very pleasing, especially when finished with a good brand of stain that allows the grain to show.

Assembly is also a source of pride with this maker. Every chair is hand-assembled using a special chair press that exerts maximum pressure to secure every joint that is subject to abuse. Pins are driven deeply into joints to lock them tightly while the special assembly glue is drying. Large posts and arms are also wedged for extra strength. These are among the least expensive of the quality hardwood chairs, yet they're built for a long, useful life.

Hardwood Imports
1600 Downs Dr., Suite 4
West Chicago, Illinois 60185
312-293-1310

Massive "Lincoln" rocker features all solid hardwood construction, $189. This is the most substantial rocker I've seen at the price.

Roll-seat "Mrs." rocker features rolled front and comfortable slat-back spindles, $70.

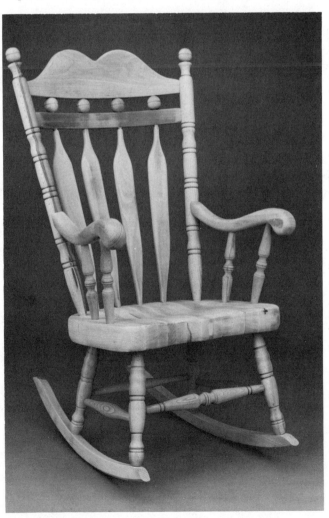

Hardwood Imports (continued)

Solid hardwood captain's chair, $75. First mate's, $50.

Slat mate's chair, $49.

Captain's bar stools, in 24″ or 30″ heights, $72.

Harris of Pendleton

Harris Pine is the largest supplier of ready-to-finish furniture in the world by far, manufacturing and shipping from ten plants across the United States. The company is owned and operated by the Seventh-Day Adventists, who provide jobs in the plants to hundreds of student Adventists. Of particular advantage to ready-to-finish customers are the overall low prices of Harris merchandise, which are in part due to the short shipping distances to most stores. Harris also sells finished furniture, which provides even more sales volume for the company. Much of the savings resulting from that volume is passed on to customers in the form of lower prices.

Harris of Pendleton
P.O. 1168
Pendleton, Oregon 97801
503-276-1421

Laurelcraft wrap group features solid alder small hutch tops, $119 each. One-drawer, two-door base cabinet, $139. Desk, $169. Three-drawer chest, $119. Corner desk, $125. Six-drawer dresser, $195. Mirror, $49.

Laurelcraft solid alder canopy group. Double dresser, $195. Mirror, $49. Canopy bed, twin size, $159. Double size, $169. Night stand, $89. Blouse chest, $229.

Harris of Pendleton (continued)

Pine Ridge group in solid pine. Armoire, $319. Night stand, $139. Bed, $195. Eight-drawer triple dresser with mirror hutch, $559 (above).

Pine River group in solid pine with carved designs. Five-drawer chest, $209. Night stand, $109. Bed, $159. Eight-drawer triple dresser with mirror, $349 (below).

Oak Harbor group in solid oak and oak veneer over particleboard. Five-drawer chest, $259. Night stand, $129. Queen bed, $229. Double dresser and tri-fold mirror, $409.

Solid alder hall tree mirror with storage, $239.

Harris of Pendleton (continued)

Solid alder hutch and buffet with glass doors, 51″ wide, $639.

Laurelcraft occasional tables in solid alder. End table, $139. Sofa table, $195. End table with door and shelves, $169. Coffee table, $159.

The Harris Pine line—the "meat and potatoes" of the ready-to-finish industry since the middle '40s. These items are in more homes than any of the furniture sold by nearly any of the other manufacturers in this book.

Five-drawer chest, $92. Four-drawer chest, $89. Three-drawer chest, $69. Night stand, $52. Five-drawer highboy chest, $71. Ten-drawer desser, $141 (opposite page).

Harris of Pendleton (continued)

Sea captain's desk in alder with pull-out writing ledge, $379.

Oak rolltop desk is 51″ wide, 47″ high, and 22″ deep, $489.

C.H. Hartshorn

Hartshorn is primarily a finished furniture supplier with limited distribution of ready-to-finish items.

C.H. Hartshorn, Inc.
562 Main Street
Gardner, Massachusetts 01440
617-632-3300

Queen Anne collection of solid northern white ash. Writing desk, $199. Oval end table, $149. Rectangular coffee table, $169.

Solid hardwood Country Collection. End table, $129. Drop-leaf cocktail table, $149.

Heirloom Enterprises

All Heirloom tables are solid northern red oak chosen for the best grain patterns. Table skirts are extra thick and screwed to each top. Simple assembly requires only a pliers. All that is needed for you to appreciate the value and sturdiness of these tables is for you to try to lift one.

Heirloom Enterprises, Inc.
County Road 1, P.O. Box 146
Dundas, Minnesota 55019
507-645-9341

Heavy antique reproductions in solid northern red oak. Round end table with turned pedestal is 30″ round, 22″ high, $199. Sofa table with double turned pedestals, 48″ long, $289. Round end table is 30″ × 22″ high, $189. Oval coffee table with double pedestals, $289.

Square end table with turned pedestal, $169. With plain pedestal, $149. Rectangular coffee tables with double pedestals, 38″ long, $219; 48″ long, $259.

Graceful, yet massive, turned pedestals. Model "A" is 34″ tall with a 14″ round top; "B" is 29″ high with a 12″ round top.

Solid wood scrolling is available on all styles and is applied to front and back of each table. Add about 5% to cost for scrolling.

High Point Woodworking

High Point Woodworking takes extra care in chair assembly to provide chairs that will hold up even under tough commercial use. Screws are used through leg dowels into the seat. Backposts are also wedged for extra strength. Tables feature tongue-and-grooved joints and carved feet. Extension tables use steel slides with ball bearings for easiest operation and rigidity. All items are made of northern and Appalachian oak, rather than the softer southern oak. Availability of these items is limited because High Point is a newcomer to the ready-to-finish specialty store market. Most stores will treat these items as special orders only.

High Point Woodworking Co., Inc.
P.O. Box 1815, Giles Street
High Point, North Carolina 27261
919-431-1139

Arm chair, $195, and side chair, $169, are solid oak.

Jamestown dining table is solid oak, 42″ wide × 60″ long, plus one 12″ leaf, $459.

Hinkle

Hinkle Chair Company products are also sold through Jackson Sales in some areas. Solid oak is the rule with Hinkle in these traditionally popular items. Hinkle merchandise is very low priced for solid oak. This is achieved through concentrating on machining the oak for use, not necessarily for decorative frills.

Hinkle Chair Company
P.O. Drawer O
Springfield, Tennessee 37172
1-800-251-3025

Solid oak 48″ round dining table features large round turned pedestal and sturdy traditional claws, $259. Solid oak chairs with woven seats. Side chair, $59. Arm chair, $69. This table can also be used very effectively with contemporary style chairs.

Solid oak extension table is 48″×72″ with two leaves. Table features large lion's paw feet, $495. I've had this table in my kitchen for the last seven years and it looks as good as the day it was finished—even with the pounding of my three kids. Embossed back chairs are also solid oak, $99.

Square-top extension has the same base and opens to 48″×72″, $495.

Hippopotamus

Hippopotamus has taken a giant leap forward in the ready-to-finish market by providing exceptionally well-designed solid oak items in the ample sizes and heavier weights first popularized on the West Coast. While the cost of these items is high as compared to the price points normally found in ready-to-finish stores, superior quality and design make these very popular with the customer who wants items to look right with other expensive furnishings. Distribution is limited to 14 western states plus the New England area; however, many dealers in other areas handle these items on a special order basis.

Hippopotamus
13162 Raymer Street
North Hollywood, California 91605
213-982-6606

Solid oak double-lip extension dining table opens to 42″×120″ with three leaves, $795. Matching pillow arm chairs, $149.

Glass-top dining table with solid oak pedestal, 36″×60″, $249. Oak parquet dining table, 36″×60″, with walnut trim, $295.

Solid oak gateleg table in 1¼″ thick butcher block opens to 36″×60″, $395.

Hippopotamus (continued)

Solid oak computer desk with hutch, $619.

Tawny Oak line of bar stools. Arm chairs with upholstery or solid oak Windsor stools with brass rings, $159.

Jorgensen

Jorgensen features heavy bullnosed trim of solid oak and finest oak veneers. Their distribution is primarily in the western states.

Jorgensen Furniture, Inc.
951 Newhall Street
Costa Mesa, California 92627
714-645-0310

Portable oak computer desk with removable CRT shelf features wiring holes and heavy duty casters, $199.

Complete home entertainment center with pull-out shelf that swivels for TV, $479.

Vertical stereo cabinet with flip-up top, $269. Large vertical stereo cabinet with pull-out shelf and storage area, $339.

Kenco—Unassembled Kit Furniture

These are the same chairs you see in fine furniture stores and decorator showrooms at substantially higher prices than you see listed here. Kenco chairs are hand-carved in Italy and are faithfully authentic replicas. Kenco chairs are available as kits only, although some dealers may be persuaded to assemble them for you. You will need clamps for assembly to do the job right. Many of these chairs will need additional sanding, particularly those with continuous carvings. Chair joints feature complete mortise and tenon construction.

Chairs with upholstered seats include a muslin and foam-covered, shaped seat that can easily be covered with your choice of needlepoint, using only a pair of shears and a stapler. Full instructions come with each chair.

Kenco chairs have very limited distribution. I suggest you contact them first for an outlet near you, or for a direct-sales catalog.

Kenco, Inc.
P.O. Box 723
Weston, Massachusetts 02193
617-623-7650

Louis XVI oval back. Popular in the 1774–1793 era. From classic Greek and Roman designs, $199.

Sheraton side and arm chairs. Solid mahogany wood in classic English design. Side chair, $225. Arm chair, $299.

Gothic Chippendale (1705–1774). Chinese-style back with straight gothic legs in solid mahogany, $299.

"Louis XV Pompadour." Intricate pierced backs exemplified Madame Pompadour's influence on furniture of this era. This chair was derived from the "Lion Masque" chair of 1735. The price is $279 in solid beech.

"Tuscany." This style evolved from a rebirth of Greek and Roman arts during the Cromwellian period. Chairs were rectangular and straight with heavy underbracing. High, narrow cane back and pierced top were of Spanish influence. The price is $149 in solid beech.

"Louis XV Roubaix." Delicate cane back design and lack of straight lines characterized furniture of this era. Solid maple version is $209.

"Country French." From the Elizabethan period, this replica is from a royal household chair. Complete with rush seat, it costs $169 in solid beech.

"Queen Anne," 1702–1714. One of the first chair designs with a back shaped to the body. Top is of Dutch influence, the leg is French cabriole. The price is $169 in solid beech.

"Torino," from the William and Mary era. Classic cane seat and solid beech construction, $159.

Kestell

Kestell is one of the largest poker and game table suppliers to the finished furniture trade. The large pedestal table has served well in the author's home for seven years. Legs and rails are in oak, birch, or maple. Tables feature mitered joints with clamp nails for secure fit. Chairs have mortise and tenon construction.

Only recently have these items been made available to ready-to-finish stores. Contact Kestell directly for a retail source.

Kestell Furniture Co., Inc.
1311 Milwaukee Drive
New Holstein, Wisconsin 53061
414-898-4251

Poker table with legs is 57″ in diameter, $195.

Large pedestal poker table is 57″ in diameter, $395.

Matching folding chairs are about $35 each. All of these tables come with eight glass ash trays.

Khoury

Khoury has been a major supplier of ready-to-finish furniture for over 30 years. Availability of these items is excellent throughout the United States. Most ready-to-finish dealers stock this line in depth or can order specific items within a few weeks. Quality is excellent when considering the very reasonable prices asked for these solid hardwood items.

Khoury, Inc.
P.O. Box 729
Iron Mountain, Michigan 49801
906-774-7208

Oak drop-lid secretary is 32″ wide, $239.

"Cortland" oak chest-on-chest, $369.

Matching bedroom items: five-drawer chest, $239. Matching headboards are also available.

Nine-drawer dresser is 62″ wide, with deck mirror, $499.

Khoury (continued)

"Cortland" oak specialty items.

Curio cabinet, 35″ wide, 57″ high, $269. Price includes glass shelves.

Baby's dressing table, $219.

The Essex County line in solid hardwood.

Solid hardwood bedroom: four-drawer chest-on-chest, 36″ wide, 52″ high, $239; nine-drawer dresser is 62″ wide, $239.

Essex County specialty items in solid hardwood.

Seven-drawer rolltop desk, $269.

Dry sink, 32″ wide, $149.

Wardrobe is 36″ wide, $199.

Lingerie chest, 54″ high, $149.

Sewing center and desk combination is 63″ wide with leaf up and 43″ wide with leaf down, $149. Sewing bench with pad, $89.

#1701, Sewing Bench (Pad Included)
20″ W × 17½″ D × 21″ H

Kroehler Cabinet

A former giant in the finished furniture industry, Kroehler Furniture began their interest in the ready-to-finish furniture industry when they bought Dawson Cabinet, maker of oak antique replicas, and renamed the company Kroehler Cabinet. Kroehler has since added many of the items shown here and has increased their distribution nationally. Kroehler has maintained the fine quality of their reproductions while continuing to provide reasonable prices.

Kroehler Cabinet Co.
P.O. Box 310
Webb City, Missouri 64870
417-673-2458

Solid oak collection:

Hutch and buffet with curved glass, $499.
Wash stand, $169.
Curved glass curio with four glass shelves, $449.

Solid oak specialty items:

Round curio with four glass shelves, $299.
Hall tree with storage, $189.

The Country Pine Collection:

Armoire, $479.

Lattice Craft

Hark back to the gracious charm of yesteryear with this Gazebo Kit featuring pressure-treated white pine in octagonal design, 10'6" in diameter. Full instructions come with this kit. All hardware is attached to the frame and panels. The only tools needed are hammer, screwdriver, and ½" wrench. Assembly time is estimated at under one hour. It is priced at around $1000.

Lattice Craft cubes, pedestals, and screens come assembled and are available in a small number of ready-to-finish stores. The gazebo is a special order item only.

Lattice Craft
527 Main Street, P.O. Box 348
Harwich, Massachusetts 02645
617-432-4022

Pine folding screens. This basket design screen is 48" × 80", $129. Also available in other sizes and designs.

Pine nested cubes are glued and stapled construction. Cubes are available in lattice design only. Sizes range from 11" cubes to 21" cubes, $19 to $39 each.

A.A. Laun
Foxborough Collection—
18th Century

Noted in the finished furniture industry for years for their heavy, solid oak and maple occasional tables, A.A. Laun has just begun to sell through ready-to-finish dealers. You may have to search a bit for a dealer who stocks these, but you won't be disappointed at the quality.

A.A. Laun
Kiel, Wisconsin 53042
414-894-7441

If you like the idea of solid maple, high styling, and reasonable cost, these should be looked at. One-drawer end table, about $220. Two-drawer lowboy, $300. Mirror, $149. Cocktail table, $249. Miniature chest (two drawers), $249.

A.A. Laun
Loyalty Oak—
Traditional

Mostly of solid oak, these are large-sized tables designed for the bulkier traditional looks. The cocktail drop-leaf table measures 40″ × 20½″ × 16″ high, and retails for about $295.

Doughbox, $289. Hexagonal commode, $289.

A.A. Laun (continued)

Drop-leaf cocktail table, $269. Butler table, $249.

A.A. Laun
Tamboura—
Transitional

Rolltop entertainment center made of solid oak
and oak veneer. It retails for about $600.

Mayline

Mayline is one of the largest suppliers of quality drafting and art cabinet furniture to specialty office furniture dealers. They have just begun to offer their fine wood products without finish for the do-it-yourselfer. Very few ready-to-finish stores will have information on Mayline yet. Write to the company to find a store in your area that can special-order these items for you.

Mayline Company, Inc.
619 N. Commerce Street
Sheboygan, Wisconsin 53081
414-457-5537

Hardwood drawing table features fully adjustable basswood top. With the 24″ × 36″ top, the table is priced at $102; with the 30″ × 42″ top, the table is $124.

"Classroom" art table has 20″ × 34″ top, hardwood base, and drawer, $264.

Classroom/hobby center features six hardwood drawers and base, and basswood adjustable top, $987.

Hardwood taboret with top well, one tool drawer and two shallow drawers, plus white plastic top, $325 (opposite page).

Hardwood plan files and drawer units. Hundreds of combinations available. Model shown is cabinet that files 30″ × 42″ papers, $1665 (opposite page).

McCoy's

You can file this under the "oddity" category in your mind, but for some unknown reason—at least to me—people actually buy this Pharaoh-sized rocker. I do know that many sales are to retailers who use it for promotional stunts—but would you buy one for your home? Some people have. If you simply *have* to have one of these you should know that this rocker is ten feet high, five feet wide, and despite its 278-pound weight, it comes with the wise advice that you should anchor it to the ground during high winds. Obviously, sails are not included. Only $2.34 per pound, the total price is $650. The only way you can buy this is to call or write the factory directly. But please do me a favor. If you buy one, please write and tell me what the heck you're doing with it.

McCoy's Furniture
R.R. #5 Box 206 A
Peru, Indiana 46970
317-689-8896

Mooney

Mooney is a long-time supplier to the ready-to-finish market mainly on the Eastern seaboard, the Gulf states, and the Midwest. The solid woods that are used are cottonwood and aspen. The veneers used are birch plywood for the case ends and luan plywood for case backs and drawer bottoms. Drawers are center-guided, with guides dadoed into the rails in front and back. Anti-spill feature requires that drawers be tilted up 30 degrees in front to remove. Nylon slides are also provided so drawers open easily.

Mooney Mfg. Co., Inc.
P.O. Box 28, Main Street
Flowery Branch, Georgia 30542
404-967-6451

Solid hardwood and hardwood veneer bedroom furniture:

Five-drawer chest, $109. Night stand, $59. Chest/robe cabinet, 48″ wide, $169. Toy chest with drawer effect, 40″ wide, $109.

Oak Crest

You needn't worry about finishing these complicated desks. Most ready-to-finish stores that carry Oak Crest sell them factory-finished in your choice of two or three stains. I've finished my share of difficult-to-finish items, but I get shivers even thinking about having to finish one of these. Distribution is national, but only in very select stores. Expect a four- to six-week waiting period for your choice of stains.

Oak Crest Manufacturing
2221 E. 49th Street
Los Angeles, California 90058
213-589-7351

It's not enough to call this a rolltop desk. Perhaps "Granddaddy" of all rolltop desks is more accurate. I have never seen a more impressive one. This desk is oak with raised beveled paneling throughout. About the drawers: they feature solid brass hardware; dovetailing; accu-ride glides; dividers in all drawers; carved wood pulls; suspended file rods in file drawers; curved doors in pigeonhole section; automatic locking when top is down; felt lining in center drawer.

Desk also features: hidden work light; mail slots; three or four secret compartments (you won't find out where until you buy the desk); two dictation slides; a safe-like compartment with lock; a place for a telephone answering device; and yes, a liquor cabinet!—underneath, behind two doors, near where your feet go.

Desk is 66″ × 36″ × 54″ high and weighs 475 pounds, $2600.

Solid oak high-back "Banker's" chair with cane seat and bentwood arm, $369. Two-drawer file, $349.

Somewhat smaller desk has many of the same features as the previously described rolltop desk, $1800.

Precision Craft

Precision Craft is one of the largest manufacturers of contemporary oak furniture. They use Appalachian solid red oak for all trim. Side and top panels are of the highest quality oak veneer over all-wood cores. Precision knock-down items are among the finest-designed furniture in the industry. All door hinges are fully adjustable. Cabinet backs are glued and stapled for rigidity. Distribution is nationwide.

Precision Craft Ltd.
10 West North Avenue
Lombard, Illinois 60148
312-627-9190

A unique combination of solid oak and walnut is featured in this bedroom. Queen-size platform bed with headboard and light bridge is priced at $769. Pier cabinets are 25″ wide × 78″ high × 19″ deep, $429 each. Six-drawer, two-door dresser is 72″ wide × 32½″ high × 19″ deep, $529.

Oak "System 33" wall system with bronze glass has solid oak doors. Each unit is 33½″ w × 78″ h × 18″ d. Prices are, from left to right, $329, $398, $269, $398, $409. Lights in cabinets are optional. Also available is a turntable pull-out kit.

Oak flip-top stereo tower, $299. Mini-stereo, $169. TV cart, $89. Stereo tower, $219.

Traditionally-styled horizontal stereo cabinet, $419. Stereo tower, $309. Each cabinet is oak veneer, with two adjustable shelves and heavy brass hardware (see opposite page).

Oak stackables can be arranged in hundreds of combinations. All are 16″ deep. Prices are: drop-lid, $139; two-door base unit, $169; top unit with glass doors, $159; open cabinet, $119; top unit with wood doors, $139; three-drawer base unit, $179. Also available is a pull-out stereo slide for $49, and a light bridge, $79 (see opposite page).

Oak computer furniture for home or office features computer terminal cabinet with drawers, $199. Computer center is 50″ w × 27″ h × 22″ d, with drawers and monitor shelf, $249. Two-door data caddy is priced at $159. All computer items are knock-down for easy customer assembly with screwdriver.

Oak room divider is 63″ wide, 72″ tall, 17″ deep for $359. Add $99 for two-door kit. Comes knock-down for simple assembly with screwdriver.

PSI Design

You can't beat PSI for just hanging around. All you do is assemble, wipe on an oil stain, and take off. Company also makes benches and rockers. Distribution is national, although you may have to write the company to find an outlet near you.

PSI Design, Inc.
5690 Valmont
Boulder, Colorado 80301
303-447-0167

The Hanging Chair kit is $29.

The Body Swing Chair kit is made of solid willow hardwood, $82.

Airplanes come in small size, $39, and large size, $49.

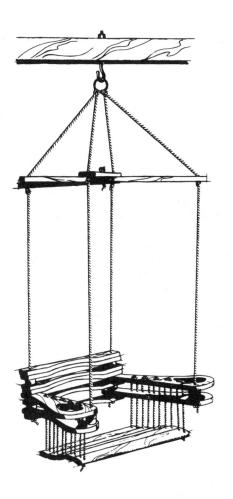

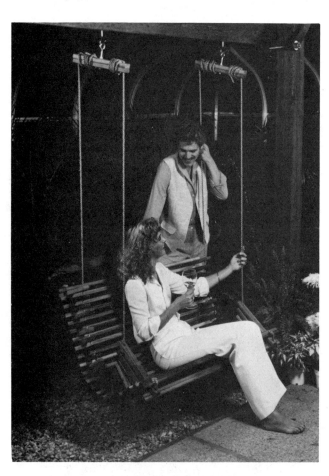

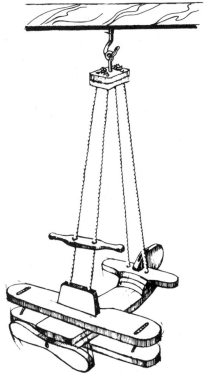

Raber

Raber Mfg. Co.
700 Third Avenue
Brooklyn, New York 11232
212-788-3818

TV cabinet with pop-top for portable TV antenna is $209 in pine, $295 in oak.

Blanket chest in solid pine is 48″ × 19¼″ × 19¼″ high, $189. The same model in oak costs $249.

Stereo cabinet with 2″ thick top in pine is 50″ × 20″ × 33″ high, features bi-fold doors, $359. The oak version is $449.

Bar cabinet is 30″ wide and features liquor storage under pop-top and two sliding wine storage trays, $299 in pine, $359 in oak.

Rex

Rex makes consistently good oak furniture year after year, concentrating on the basic items. I can personally attest to the quality of their chairs because I've had eight of their ladderbacks in my dining room for the last nine years and they're still beautiful. Rex is distributed nationally and is easily available from most ready-to-finish stores.

Rex Furniture Company, Inc.
Box 488, 3738 Rex Road
Rex, Georgia 30273
404-474-8701

Oak extension table opens to 48″ × 64″ and features an oak veneer top with solid oak edge and solid oak turned pedestal, $499. Solid oak chairs feature one-piece steam bent posts and woven seats. Side chair, $99. Arm chair, $119. Large oak hutch and buffet, $829.

Matching oak corner cabinet, $579. Oak dry sink/server, $329.

Country bow back chair in solid oak, $99. Solid oak embossed antique replica, $139. Solid oak panelback chair, $99. Colonial spindleback chair in solid oak, $89. Jumbo solid oak rocker with woven fiber seat, $239 (opposite page).

Richardson

Richardson continues to create trend-setting furniture for the ready-to-finish market. Although primarily making the finished product, Richardson has experienced tremendous acceptance by the ready-to-finish customer who is looking for the best quality solid oak tables and chairs. Distribution is national through specialty ready-to-finish stores.

Richardson Brothers Co.
P.O. Box 157
Sheboygan Falls, Wisconsin 53085
414-467-4631

Solid oak dining set features country oak hutch/buffet that serves as a desk, bar or curio, $1395. Double-pedestal extension table opens to 50" × 35" oval. The 18" leaf is stored under the table top. Table features self-leveling glides, equalizing slides, and easy one-side finger lock mechanism, $729. Solid oak chair, $109.

Solid oak bentwood oval pedestal table opens to 41" × 64" with four 11" self-storing leaves, $795.

Contemporary solid oak bow back arm chair, $199. Side chair, $139 (opposite page).

Solid oak double-pedestal table opens to 47"× 69" with two 11" fills, $775 (opposite page).

Matching solid oak chairs: Paddle arm chair, $199. Side chair, $159 (opposite page).

Solid oak country table is 41" × 59" with leaf, $529. Solid oak bow back captain's chair, $159. Mate's chair (not shown), $139 (opposite page).

Unique solid oak corner cabinet serves as bar or curio, $1350. Base unit available separately for $759 (opposite page).

Robinson's

With its own sawmill in the middle of Michigan's upper peninsula, Robinson has first pick of the best of the northern hardwoods, primarily oak. Robinson's has been a leading supplier of rockers and dining room furniture to the finished furniture industry for 25 years. In the last few years, Robinson's oak furniture has gotten the increased attention of the ready-to-finish furniture dealers, largely because of the ample use of thick oak stock in most of their items. Distribution of their ready-to-finish line is national, although concentrated in the middle states.

Robinson's Furniture Mfg., Inc.
Box 94
Wilson, Michigan 49896
906-639-2151

Solid oak dinette table is 36″ × 48″, $265. Solid oak side chair, $94.

Solid oak hutch and buffet, 50″ wide, 18″ deep, $1070.

Solid oak desk/table with drawers, 36″ × 60″, $388. Solid oak side chair, $103.

Solid oak double-pedestal table is 48″ round and opens to 72″ with two leaves, $778. The same table with four leaves opens to 96″ for $890. Solid oak side chair, $134; arm chair, $167 (see opposite page).

"Harvest Oak" swing rockers (pictured on opposite page).

Traditional solid oak rocker, $288.

Bow back with flat slats, $332.

Bent arms with cushions, $377.

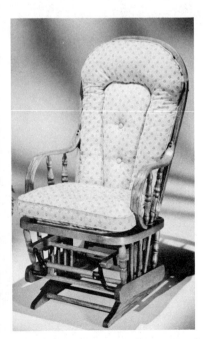

Sonoma

Sonoma is a leading manufacturer of contemporary-styled, knock-down, ready-to-finish furniture. They take particular care to machine all wood parts to very close tolerances. This provides for a perfect fit when assembling. Metal-to-metal connectors are used throughout for easy customer assembly. Complete instructions are packed with each carton. I've used Sonoma for my customers for over ten years and I'm still impressed with the way they follow up on customer complaints with their fast factory service on replacement parts. Sonoma is available nationwide through ready-to-finish specialty stores. Allow four to six weeks on special fabric orders.

Sonoma
P.O. Box 1009
Rohnert Park, California 94928
707-584-7680

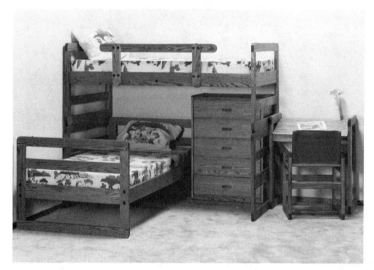

Glass top dining group available in oak or pine. Easy customer assembly required. Table is 56″ × 35″ × 30″ and is priced at $279 in oak, $169 in pine. Chairs are $109 in oak, $69 in pine. There are eight fabric choices with oak, six with pine.

Loft bed that converts to twin beds is available in oak or pine, $599/oak, $319/pine. Desk with lift-up top is $159/oak, $119/pine. Chair, $99/$69. Five-drawer chest, $319/$299.

"Cascade" four-drawer desk is priced at $129 in oak only. Five-drawer chest costs $319 in oak, $299 in pine.

"Cascade" bedroom group is available in oak or pine. The set features a unique chest bed, $419 in oak, $339 in pine. Other items in oak/pine are: six-drawer dresser, $329/$319; double hutch, $109/$99; night stand, $99/$89; mirror, $89/$79.

Solid oak seating group features metal-to-metal connectors for easy customer assembly. Polyfoam cushions are available in a full selection of fabric colors, grades, and styles. The sofa costs $449; loveseat, $319; chair, $219; coffee table, $129; console, $199; five-shelf etagère, $229; four-shelf etagère, $199; three-shelf etagère, $159.

Tubb

Since 1896, Tubb has made spokes, bows, rims, and the bent and turned parts for wagon wheels. They began making chairs decades ago and continue to be a quality producer for ready-to-finish specialty stores. The chairs pictured represent nearly their entire selection. What they make they make exceedingly well. If you want authentically-styled, down-home solid oak chairs, these are the ones to ask for. Distribution is national through specialty stores.

Tubb Woodcrafters
North Davidson Street
Tullahoma, Tennessee 37388
615-455-0705

Solid oak Governor Carver side chair, $99.

Matching arm chair, $159.

Solid oak American Windsor side chair, $119.

Matching arm chair, $169.

Solid oak Governor Carver swivel desk chair, $219.

Solid oak American Windsor swivel desk chair, $229.

Union City

Union City Chair has been the "meat and potatoes" chair line of most ready-to-finish stores.
They have consistently offered well-made solid
hardwood chairs at the lowest prices of any
other manufacturer. Their latest entry into oak
items has been particularly well received. Union
City enjoys probably the widest distribution of
any other ready-to-finish chair maker, so you
won't have to look far to see these items.

Union City Chair Company
18 Market Street
Union City, Pennsylvania 16438
814-438-3878

Solid oak drop-leaf table is 42″ round, $155.
Oak bow back chairs, $59.

Solid oak drop-leaf table is 44″ × 36″, $140.
Oak spear back chairs, $59.

Solid hardwood embossed chairs, choice of
styles, $79.

Solid hardwood bow back high chair with tray,
$65.

Union City (continued)

Nostalgic hardwood bow back chair is nearly identical to the original model made by Union City in 1906. The original retail price was about 95 cents. The circa 1983 chair is $35.

Solid hardwood bend-arm rocker with embossed back, $135.

Walton

Walton was one of the earliest companies to produce quality home entertainment furniture for ready-to-finish stores. Their computer furniture is exceptionally well designed. Walton has a wide distribution, especially in the states surrounding Texas.

Walton Furniture Industries, Inc.
1400 Turtle Creek Boulevard
Dallas, Texas 75207
214-748-8777

Electronic center in oak veneer with solid oak trim has room for home computer plus TV monitor and more. Unit is 60″ wide, 72″ high, 17″ deep, $459.

Entertainment center is the same size as electronic center, but with VCR shelf under TV space and three large storage sections behind bottom doors, $299.

Computer stations in oak veneer with solid oak trim. Monitor and keyboard cabinet is 30″ wide, 17″ deep, 36″ high, for $150. Printer stand with shelf costs $100.

Computer desk is 60″ wide, 24″ deep, 26″ high, with monitor platform, $259. Smaller 48″ wide desk and platform, $229.

Western Reserve—Kit Furniture

Western Reserve sells only through their catalog.

Western Reserve Antique Furniture Kit
P.O. Box 206A
Bath, Ohio 44210

For lovers of the austere Shaker style, Western kits include everything you'll need.

Shaker drop-leaf table, $149.95 in pine; $239.95 in solid cherry; $449.95 in solid walnut. Assembly: approximately three hours.

Shaker trestle table, $134.95 in pine and birch; $199.95 in solid cherry; $329.95 in solid walnut. Assembly: approximately one and one-half hours.

Whitaker

Whitaker is a popular supplier for ready-to-finish specialty stores. Their solid oak furniture is both well made and reasonably priced. Distribution is national, but concentrated in the south and southeastern states.

Whitaker Manufacturing Co., Inc.
Searcy, Arkansas 72143
501-268-5377

Solid oak table is 36″ × 48″ × 60″ with one leaf, $309. Upholstered solid oak side chairs, $69.

Solid oak table is 42″ round plus 12″ leaf, $329. Cane back solid oak side chair, $139. Arm chair, $149.

Williams Bros.

Williams Bros. is one of the early California manufacturers of ready-to-finish furniture, beginning in 1947. They are totally dedicated to building the finest solid oak furniture in the country. Besides the items shown, they also have a wide selection of solid oak office desks, computer furniture, and occasional furniture. The company has national distribution through specialty stores, but availability of their entire line is concentrated in stores in the West Coast states.

Williams Bros. Furniture
13838 South Figueroa Street
Los Angeles, California 90061
213-324-2631

Solid oak California bedroom suites.

Night stand tower is 26″ wide, 78″ high, 17″ deep, $419. Light bridge and bookcase headboard in queen size, $399; in king size, $439.

Armoire with two adjustable shelves is 38″ wide, 66″ high, 18″ deep, $659. Triple dresser with six drawers and two trays is 74″ wide, 30″ high, 17″ deep, $679. Mirror, $119. Night stand, $195.

This solid oak set has softly rounded edges with built-in drawer pulls. All drawers are dust proof, with easy-glide nylon guides. Sides and backs are made of solid oak. Plate mirror has fully finished back.

Solid oak California modern wall systems.

Large two-door chest, $195; small two-door chest, $139; one-drawer desk, $139; bookshelves from $30 to $50.

Drop-front desk, $179; large two-door chest with glass doors, $195; three-drawer chest, $289; long vertical wall brackets, $19 each.

Oak rolltop desk is 60″ wide with raised panels, file drawers, and lots of cubbyhole drawers, $1395.

Wood's Edge

Wood's Edge is a relatively new supplier to the ready-to-finish market, but has been widely accepted because of their careful attention to quality and modest pricing for an oak product.

Wood's Edge, Inc.
P.O. Box 706
Grand Haven, Michigan 49417
616-846-1620

Oak china cabinet top with two sliding glass doors, $289. Buffet base with two drawers and two doors is 42″ wide, 18″ deep, $402. Total height is 72″.

Oak parquet extension table in chevron design opens to 36″ × 72″ with two 18″ leaves, $569. Matching solid oak chairs with curved backs and oatmeal upholstery, $115 each.

Yield House—Kit Furniture

Yield House is one of the most successful direct marketing furniture companies. This is because their furniture is well made, easy to assemble, and comes with excellent directions. If you're stumped on an assembly problem you can call the company and receive helpful advice. They feature over one hundred furniture items in their Fall '83 catalog—all of them in money-saving kit and ready-to-finish form. Yield House sells through their catalog and their retail stores in several New England states.

Yield House
Route 16
North Conway, New Hampshire 03860
1-800-258-4720

"Deerfield" computer desk comes in 11 pieces that can be assembled in about an hour and a half, $139.95.

Hidden "Exeter" computer desk fits neatly behind four doors. Comes in 56 pieces and needs approximately three hours to assemble, $349.95.

WHERE TO BUY

THIS IS A STATE-BY-STATE index of over 700 retail locations specializing in ready-to-finish furniture. Since there are many changes occurring monthly as stores move, open new outlets, change phone numbers, etcetera, I recommend that you get the phone company's latest number for the store nearest you.

While this is probably the most complete retail store index available for this industry, I'm sure there are many stores inadvertently omitted.

So please check your local classified telephone directory under "Furniture, Unfinished" and "Furniture, Retail."

Besides the several manufacturers listed in chapter four who sell direct to consumers with their catalogs, additional catalogs to check are those by Sears, Montgomery Ward's, and J.C. Penney's.

Most of the manufacturers featured in chapter four are well known to the specialty retailers listed here. By knowing the manufacturer, the specific item you're looking for, and its price, you will be able to do a great deal of shopping by telephone.

Also remember to check the prices of your local home centers and discount stores.

State-by-State Index of Ready-to-Finish Furniture Stores

ALABAMA

Unpainted Furniture Co.	1719 Crestwood Blvd.	Birmingham	AL
Unpainted Furniture Co.	2304 Center Point Rd.	Birmingham	AL
Unpainted Furniture Co.	1336 Alford Ave.	Birmingham	AL
Unfinished Shopper	3759 Ross Clark Circle N.W.	Dothan	AL
Ron's Original Wood Shop	2154 Airport Blvd.	Mobile	AL
The Wood Shed	1812 Bear Fork Rd.	Mobile	AL
Wood Au Naturel	6491 Government Blvd.	Mobile	AL
McLendon Furniture	205 Eastern Bypass	Montgomery	AL

ALASKA

The Woodbarn	5700 Old Seward Hwy.	Anchorage	AK
R.K. Unfinished Furniture	3116 Mountain View Dr.	Anchorage	AK
Unfinished Furniture Store	514 Muldoon Rd.	Anchorage	AK
Unfinished Furniture Store	2 Plaza	Anchorage	AK

ARIZONA

Earl's U-Finish Furniture	933 E. Main	Mesa	AZ
The Knot House	734 W. Main St.	Mesa	AZ
All Wood Furniture Co.	1515 E. Thomas Rd.	Phoenix	AZ
Bare Wood Shop	3619 E. Indian Schl. Rd.	Phoenix	AZ
Bill's Unfinished Furniture	4825 N. 27 Ave.	Phoenix	AZ
Bing's Furn	4536 N. 7th	Phoenix	AZ
Modern Wall Systems	20 E. Camelback Rd.	Phoenix	AZ
Orchid Interiors & Furnishings	13430 N. 7th St.	Phoenix	AZ
Naked Furniture	918 W. Camelback Rd.	Phoenix	AZ
Prestige Homes	4548 E. Van Buren	Phoenix	AZ
The Wood Shed	4222 W. Dunlap Ave.	Phoenix	AZ
For Woodness Sake	2080 E. University Dr.	Tempe	AZ
Naked Furniture	3136 S. McClintock	Tempe	AZ
Furniture in the Raw	4151 E. Speedway Blvd.	Tucson	AZ
Knock of Wood Unfinished	5030 E. Speedway Blvd.	Tucson	AZ
Westwoods of Yuma	1430 Ave. B	Yuma	AZ

ARKANSAS

Paul's Furniture Store	292 N.E. Front St.	Ashdown	AR
Wood 'n Needle	1011 Gee St.	Jonesville	AR
Unpainted Furniture Center	Univ. Plaza Shopping Plaza	Little Rock	AR
Unpainted Furniture Center	4550 John F. Kennedy Blvd.	N. Little Rock	AR
Phipp's Unpainted Furniture	116 N. Arkansas	Russellville	AR
Syjak's Unfinished Furniture	800 S. Hwy. 71	Springdale	AR

CALIFORNIA

Natural Woods Unfinished Furniture	7147 Amethyst Ave.	Alta Loma	CA
Fowler's Woodcraft Unfinished Furniture	850 E. Tregallas Rd.	Antioch	CA
Biscay's Nude Furniture Center	701 30th	Bakersfield	CA
Val's Unfinished Furniture Mfg.	4420 Santa Ana	Bell	CA
Abbott's World of Wood	17450 S. Bellflower Blvd.	Bellflower	CA
Hail's Family Furniture	17233 Clark Ave.	Bellflower	CA
Berkeley Sleep Shop	2970 Adeline St.	Berkeley	CA
J. Gorman & Son, Inc.	2599 Telegraph Ave.	Berkeley	CA
Jayco Unfinished Furniture	516 N. Victory Blvd.	Burbank	CA
Froch's Woodcraft Shop	6659 Topanga Canyon Blvd.	Canoga Park	CA
Pinocchio's Unfinished Furniture	2616 El Camino Real	Carlsbad	CA
In the Raw Furniture	P.O. Box 221487	Carmel	CA
Furniture in the Raw	6801 Westmore Way	Carmichael	CA
G.P. Unfinished Furniture Store	686 First St.	Cathedral City	CA
Oak Etc. Unfinished Furniture	12428 Running Dr. Ln.	Cerritos	CA
Dal World	228 Sunvalley Mall	Concord	CA
Woodcellar	782 N. Main	Corona	CA
Furniture in the Nude	1819 Newport Blvd.	Costa Mesa	CA
Wood World Nude Furniture	8025 Gravenstein Hwy.	Cotati	CA
Culver Ready for Finish Furniture	4366 Sepulveda Blvd.	Culver City	CA
Modern Furniture	1901 Junipero Serra Blvd.	Daly City	CA
Oak Plus	966 N. Diamond Bar Blvd.	Diamond Bar	CA
Posey's Unpainted Furniture	12639 S. Lakewood Blvd.	Downey	CA
Haywood's Unfinished Furniture	456 N. Magnolia Ave.	El Cajon	CA
Pinocchio's Unfinished Furniture	846 Fletcher Pkwy.	El Cajon	CA
Unfinished Furniture Center	23740 El Toro Rd.	El Toro	CA
The Wood Shop	618 N. Broadway	Escondido	CA
The Wood Shop	330 N. Main Ave.	Fallbrook	CA
Saddleback Wood Products	8646 Beech Ave.	Fontana	CA
Nude Furniture	40900 Fremont Blvd.	Fremont	CA
K–C's World of Wood	3251 N. Cedar Ave.	Fresno	CA
Unfinished Furniture World	3310 E. Belmont Ave.	Fresno	CA
Michael's Unfinished Furniture	1644 University Blvd.	Hillcrest	CA
Bear Wood Furniture	7551 Sunset Blvd.	Hollywood	CA
Ideal Unfinished Furniture	1018 N. Western Ave.	Hollywood	CA
Al's Woodcraft	2656 Browning Ave.	Irvine	CA
House of Unfinished Furniture	1043 N. Hacienda Bl.	La Puente	CA
Finishing Touch, Etc.	3837 Emerald Ave.	La Verne	CA
Bare in the Woods Unfinished Furniture	Hwy. 189	Lake Arrowhead	CA
Unfinished Forest	901 S. Main St.	Lakeport	CA
Creative Furniture	1332 Gladys Ave.	Long Beach	CA
Furniture in the Nude	4310 Atlantic Ave.	Long Beach	CA

CALIFORNIA (con't.)

Froch's Woodcraft Shop	7921 Beverly Blvd.	Los Angeles	CA
Status Table Mfg.	2313 E. 51st St.	Los Angeles	CA
Westside Unpainted Furniture	10205 Venice Blvd. 6	Los Angeles	CA
Little House of Nude Furniture	2359 S. Robertson Blvd.	Los Angeles	CA
Bare Wood Furniture	159 W. Main	Merced	CA
Hoot Judkins Unfinished Furniture	339 Broadway	Millbrae	CA
Natural Woods	930 N. Carpenter Rd.	Modesto	CA
The Wood Works	704 1st	Modesto	CA
Natural Wood Unfinished Furniture	5640 Monreno	Montclair	CA
Nude Furniture	1297 El Camino Real W.	Mountain View	CA
Design Depot Furnishings	P.O. Box 198	Mt. Shasta	CA
Waterbeds Bedchamber	5817 Watt Ave.	N. Highlands	CA
The Woodmill Ready-to-Finish Furniture	3250 California Blvd.	Napa	CA
Wood Mill	P.O. Box 3317	Napa	CA
The Naked Woods	576 Searls Ave.	Nevada City	CA
Rediger's Valley Furniture	11252 Magnolia Blvd.	North Hollywood	CA
Bare Facts Unfinished Furniture	1425 Grant Ave.	Novato	CA
Krisjou Unfinished Furniture	1411 N. Hill	Oceanside	CA
Froch's Woodcraft Shop	7945 Van Nuys Blvd.	Panorama City	CA
Bartlett's Ready-to-Finish	3725 E. Colorado Blvd.	Pasadena	CA
The Woodshop	1040 13th	Paso Robles	CA
Petaluma Nude Shop	800 Petaluma Blvd. S.	Petaluma	CA
All Bare Furniture Factory	50 Main St.	Placerville	CA
Fowler's Unfinished Furniture	2346 Monument Blvd.	Pleasant Hill	CA
The Saw Mill, Inc.	2316 Monument Blvd.	Pleasant Hill	CA
The Wood House	1091 W. Linda Vis Ave.	Porterville	CA
The Final Touch	13931 Midland Rd.	Poway	CA
Nude Rat	155 Ford	Redlands	CA
Graham & Son Unfinished Furniture	101 N. Pacific Coast Hwy.	Redondo Beach	CA
Royal Creations	9120 Center St.	Rancho Cucamonga	CA
Copenhagen	1018 J St.	Sacramento	CA
Earle's Unfinished Furniture	541 Munroe St.	Sacramento	CA
Naked Furniture	2265 Watt Ave.	Sacramento	CA
Naturwood Furniture	4300 Stockton Blvd.	Sacramento	CA
Nude Furniture	4622 Auburn Blvd.	Sacramento	CA
Hoot Judkins Unfinished Furniture	1400 El Camino Real	San Bruno	CA
Acadia Unfinished Furniture Mart	5255 University Ave.	San Diego	CA
Bare Woods	4678 Alvarado Cnyn. Rd.	San Diego	CA
Bob Haywood's Unfinished Furniture	4475 Mercury St.	San Diego	CA
Pinocchio's Unfinished Furniture	1130 W. Morena Blvd.	San Diego	CA
Specialty Furniture Shop	2885 El Cajon Blvd.	San Diego	CA
Wood Please	803 W. Harbor Dr.	San Diego	CA

CALIFORNIA (con't.)

Woody's Unfinished Furniture	4475 Mercury St.	San Diego	CA
Ace Unfinished Furniture Co.	1825 Polk	San Francisco	CA
Chair Store	701 Bayshore Blvd.	San Francisco	CA
Country Living	1033 Clement	San Francisco	CA
Decor Unfinished Furniture	1899 W. San Carlos	San Jose	CA
Wood 'n Stuff	718 S. Rancho Santa Fe Rd.	San Marcos	CA
San Rafael Woodworks	825 Francisco Blvd. W.	San Rafael	CA
Wood Factory	3001 S. Crody Way	Santa Ana	CA
Ye Old Wood Shoppe, Inc.	5156 Hollister Ave.	Santa Barbara	CA
Santa Rosa Bare Woods	966 Piner Rd.	Santa Rosa	CA
World of Carpets & Home Furniture	3023 Santa Rosa Ave.	Santa Rosa	CA
Gary's Finishing Touch	10251 Mast Bl.	Santee	CA
Brooks' Furniture	15122 Ventura Blvd.	Sherman Oaks	CA
In the Woods Furniture	908 W. Highland Ave.	San Bernardino	CA
Mr. Good Wood	18969 Sonoma Hwy.	Sonoma	CA
Sweets in the Nude	3131 Soquel Dr.	Soquel	CA
Cousyn's Unfinished Furniture	7520 Katella Ave.	Stanton	CA
Woodworks II	4593 Central Way	Suison City	CA
Bare Wood	168 E. Fremont	Sunnyvale	CA
Nude Furniture	1297 El Camino Real W.	Sunnyvale	CA
Woodworks	760 N. Lake Blvd.	Tahoe City	CA
The Wood Shop	1945 Campbell	Thousand Oaks	CA
The Wood Shop	688 N. Moorpark Rd.	Thousand Oaks	CA
Unfinished Furniture Mart	2539 Pacific Coast Hwy.	Torrance	CA
Modern Way Furniture	20319 Hawthorn Blvd.	Torrance	CA
Al's Woodcraft	1471 Nissou Rd.	Tustin	CA
Miller's Unfinished Furniture	6339 Adobe Rd.	Twenty-Nine Palm	CA
Bill's Furniture Factree	125 N. Mountain	Upland	CA
Woodealer	2517 Beniss Rd.	Valdosta	CA
Elliot's Unfinished Furniture	925 N. Ventura Ave.	Ventura	CA
Unfinished Furniture	4013 E. Main	Ventura	CA
The Finishing Touch	26644 S. Mooney Blvd.	Visalia	CA
The Wood Shop	416 E. Vista Way	Vista	CA
David's House of Unfinished Furniture	1530 Olympic Blvd.	Walnut Creek	CA
The Wood Factory	107 Westminster Mall	Westminster	CA
Marinello's Unfinished Furniture	7124 Mohawk Tr. #C	Yucca Valley	CA

CANADA

Modern Woodcraft Mfg., Ltd.	4482 Dawson St.	Burnaby, British Columbia	CN
Alberta Wood Products	211 17th Ave. S.E.	Calgary, Alberta	CN

CANADA (con't.)

Woodcroft Furniture Ltd.	2228 Ave. C North	Saskatoon, Saskatchewan	CN
Davis-Craft Furniture Mfg., Ltd.	2779 Commercial	Vancouver, British Columbia	CN
W.L. Factory Showroom	548 W. Broadway	Vancouver, British Columbia	CN

COLORADO

Contemporary Comfort	4747 Pearl St.	Boulder	CO
Kellert Unfinished Furniture	2885 30th	Boulder	CO
The Denver Warehouse	1801 N. Union Blvd.	Colorado Springs	CO
Finishing Touch, Inc.	309 6th	Crested Butte	CO
Colorado Building Specialty	11000 E. 40th Ave.	Denver	CO
Naked Furniture	5461 S. Salida St.	Denver	CO
Unpainted Furniture	1601 S. Colorado Blvd.	Denver	CO
Tinkerwood	701 W. Hampden Ave. Ci.	Englewood	CO
Dobbi House	728 Cooper Ave.	Glenwood Springs	CO
Wood Interiors	2962 North Ave.	Grand Junction	CO
Naked Furniture of Littletown	2539 W. Main	Littletown	CO
Bargain House Furniture	1125 Francis St.	Longmont	CO
Longmont U-Finish Furniture	1106 Main	Longmont	CO
Unpainted Furniture Center	9830 W. I–70	Wheatridge	CO

CONNECTICUT

Bob's Unfinished Furniture	429 Post Rd.	Darien	CT
Pinewood Furniture Shop	379 E. Center Rd.,	Manchester	CT
Huckleberry Finn	Connecticut Post Mall	Milford	CT
Unfinished Furniture House	59 John Fitch Blvd	South Windsor	CT
Jim's Unfinished Furniture	198 Henry	Stamford	CT
Woodcraft Unlimited, Inc.	1007 High Ridge Rd.	Stamford	CT
Naked Furniture	1099 New Britain Ave.	West Hartford	CT
Woodworks	557 New Park Ave.	West Hartford	CT
Williams Unpainted Furniture	732 Silas Deane Hwy.	Wethersfield	CT
Pine Knot Unfinished Furniture	445 Main St.	Willimantic	CT

DELAWARE

Mar–Stan's Unpainted Furniture	Chestnut Hill Plz.	Newark	DE

FLORIDA

Nude Oak Furniture	808 N. Ridgewood Ave.	Daytona Beach	FL
Naked Furniture	8530 State Rd.	Fort Lauderdale	FL

FLORDIA (con't.)

Le Vay's Unfinished Furniture	1515 S.E. 47th Terr.	Fort Myers	FL
Le Vay's Unpainted Furniture	1821 Paul St.	Fort Myers	FL
Naked Furniture	5306 Cleveland	Fort Myers	FL
The Wood Shed	6305 S. Federal Hwy.	Fort Pierce	FL
Nina's Nook	818 W. University Ave.	Gainesville	FL
Country Heritage Furniture	1313 N. Ridgewood	Holly Hill	FL
Solid Wood to Go	3626 Beach Blvd.	Jacksonville	FL
Wood You	8309 Atlantic Blvd.	Jacksonville	FL
Wood You	230 S. Edgewood Ave.	Jacksonville	FL
Wood You 2	5032 Normandy Blvd.	Jacksonville	FL
Heddon Wood Products Company	P.O. Box 3416	Lake Wales	FL
Almin Furniture	1920 Lake Worth Rd.	Lake Worth	FL
Nude & Natural Unfinished Furniture	4920 N. 10th Ave.	Lake Worth	FL
Country Heritage	1605 Bartow Rd.	Lakeland	FL
Waterbedroom, Inc.	3465 N.W. 19th St. Bldg.	Lauderdale Lake	FL
Blackwelder's	2653 N. State Rd. #7	Lauderhill	FL
Village Sawmill	329 N. Babcock St.	Melbourne	FL
Blackwelder's Furniture	18810 S. Dixie Hwy.	Miami	FL
Lindsley Home Care Centers	8405 N.W. 53rd St.	Miami	FL
Furniture in the Buff, Inc.	940 Central Ave.	Naples	FL
Nude Oak, Etc.	515 Canal St.	New Smyrna Beach	FL
Wood Your Way	1011 N.E. 14th St.	Ocala	FL
Camplighter Antiques & Furniture	1333 Brookhaven Dr.	Orlando	FL
Lane's Orange Avenue Furniture	2307-09 S. Orange Ave.	Orlando	FL
Du-It Ur-Self Un-Finished Furniture	427 S. Nova Rd.	Ormond Beach	FL
The Unfinished Shoppe	5306 E. Business Hwy. 98	Panama City	FL
Knock on Wood	6923-A North 9th Ave.	Pensacola	FL
Furniture in the Buff, Inc.	6528 S. Tamiami	Sarasota	FL
Lane's Furniture	1108 New York Ave.	St. Cloud	FL
The Wood Shed	4440 S. Federal Hwy.	Stuart	FL
Scan House	1416 Timberland Rd.	Tallahassee	FL
Naked Furniture	1218-20 Fowler Ave.	Tampa	FL
Trader's Mart	2018 Commerce Ave.	Vero Beach	FL

GEORGIA

Home Depot	4380 Memorial Dr.	Decatur	GA
Home Depot	5600 Buford Hwy.	Doraville	GA
Home Depot	3850 Jonesboro Rd.	Forest Park	GA
Home Depot	1901 Terrell Mill Rd. S.E.	Marietta	GA
The Unfinished Furniture Store	Power's Ferry Rd.	Marietta	GA
Design House International	6348 N.E. Expressway	Norcross	GA

GEORGIA (con't.)

Unfinished Furniture	537 Smith Ave.	Thomasville	GA
Bare Wood Furniture Co.	841 E. Currahee	Toccoa	GA
Wood-U-Finish	1218 Rockbridge Rd.	Tucker	GA
Unfinished Fashion Furniture	1111 3rd Ave.	West Point	GA

HAWAII

Paulette's Furniture, Inc.	314 Keawe	Hawaii	HI
The Wooden Stitch	49 Kaahumanu Ave.	Kahului Maui	HI
Nude Shop/Maui Mini Storage	9914 Limahana Pl.	Lahaina	HI
Your Finishing Touch of Maui	1013 Limahana Pl.	Lahaina	HI
Shin Furniture Co.	1269 S. Beretania	Oahu	HI

IDAHO

Aunt Suzin Unfinished Furniture	5825 Glenwood	Boise	ID
Dunkley's Wood Warehouse	5321 Emerald St.	Boise	ID
Overland Decorating Center	4005 Overland	Boise	ID
Wood 'n Things	3610 E. Cleveland Blvd.	Caldwell	ID
Romaine's House of Color	401 E St.	Idaho Falls	ID
Furniture West	1114 Pullman Rd.	Moscow	ID

ILLINOIS

Wood Mill Unfinished	2604 State	Alton	IL
Design, Etc.	715 W. Algonquin Rd.	Arlington Hts.	IL
Naked Furniture	1802 N. Arlington Hts. Rd.	Arlington Hts.	IL
Naked Furniture	254 E. Indian Trial	Aurora	IL
Furniture Factory of Belleville	615 S. Belt W.	Belleville	IL
Naked Furniture	160 E. Lake St.	Bloomingdale	IL
The Furniture Factory	1275 Dundee Rd.	Buffalo Grove	IL
Furniture Flair	54 N. Western Rt. 31	Carpentersville	IL
Unfinished Unfinished	518 6th	Charleston	IL
A–1 Unpainted Furniture Mart	7550 N. Milwaukee	Chicago	IL
Gothic Craft	2601 W. Armitage	Chicago	IL
Gothic Craft Corp.	4862 W. Irving Pk.	Chicago	IL
Gothic Craft Corp.	933 W. Belmont	Chicago	IL
Naked Furniture	806 N. Clark St.	Chicago	IL
The Furniture Factory	2534 N. Clark St.	Chicago	IL
The Wooden Touch	1145 W. Grand Ave.	Decatur	IL
Naked Furniture	1411 Ellinwood	Des Plaines	IL
Naked Furniture	237 Ogden Ave.	Downers Grove	IL
Naked Furniture	1002 Chicago Ave.	Evanston	IL
Naked Furniture	18353 S. Halsted	Glenwood	IL

ILLINOIS (con't.)

Bare Furniture	950 W. Irving Park Rd.	Hanover Park	IL
Naked Furniture	2018 W. Jefferson	Joliet	IL
Naked Furniture	1338 S. Milwaukee Ave.	Libertyville	IL
The Wood Shed	1221 W. Jackson	Macomb	IL
Courtesy Home Center	740 E. Rand Rd.	Mt. Prospect	IL
Naked Furniture	1032 Ogden Ave.	Naperville	IL
Naked Furniture	7349 W. 25th St. N. Riverside	North Riverside	IL
Naked Furniture	Norridge Commons	Norridge	IL
The Furniture Factory	1038 W. Lake	Oak Park	IL
Dare to Go Bare	757 Pfingsten	Northbrook	IL
Dave's Unfinished Furniture	14655 S. La Grange Rd.	Orland Park	IL
Bare Furniture	756 E. Northwest Hwy.	Palatine	IL
Garden House	1707 Rand Rd.	Palatine	IL
Naked Furniture	4234 N. Brandywine	Peoria	IL
Naked Furniture	U.S. 51 and Wenzel Rd.	Peru	IL
Holly's Unfinished Furniture Center	Rural Route 30	Plainfield	IL
Naked Furniture	109 N. Alpine	Rockford	IL
The Wood House	2809 S. 6th	Springfield	IL
Custom Furniture	6 N. 518 Highway 25	St. Charles	IL
Bare Furniture	505 E. St. Charles Rd.	Villa Park	IL
Naked Furniture	140 W. North Ave.	Villa Park	IL
Knock on Wood	Hwy. 120	Volo	IL
Fopal, Inc.	Rt. 3	W. Frankfort	IL
Naked Furniture	1601 N. Main	Wheaton	IL
The Furniture Factory	100 Skokie Blvd.	Wilmette	IL

INDIANA

Wood Stock Unfinished Furniture	112 S. College	Bloomington	IN
The Woodshed	3417 1st Ave.	Evansville	IN
Naked Furniture	401 E. Coliseum Blvd.	Fort Wayne	IN
Naked Furniture	1001 U.S. 31 South	Greenwood	IN
Unfinished Furniture Co.	6302 E. 82nd Castleton	Indianapolis	IN
Naked Furniture	8402 E. Washington	Indianapolis	IN
Unfinished Furniture Factory	4919 W. 38th	Indianapolis	IN
Naked Furniture	5512 E. 82nd St.	Indianapolis	IN
Unfinished Furniture Center	Youngstown Shopping Center	Jeffersonville	IN
Naturally Now	113 N. 36th St.	Lafayette	IN
Naked Furniture	7590 Broadway P.O. Box 7206	Merrillville	IN
McCoy's Unfinished Furniture	Rural Route 5	Peru	IN
The Country Touch	715 Whitestown Rd.	Zionsville	IN

IOWA

Knot Finished Shoppe	4444 1st Ave. N.E.	Cedar Rapids	IA
The Woodpecker Shop	1081 Main St.	Dubuque	IA
Finishing Touch	107 W. Washington	Fairfield	IA
Past Recollections	51 E. Low St.	Fairfield	IA
Le Sac Interior	705 Oakhill Dr.	Sac City	IA
Wood Works	510 5 St.	Sioux City	IA
Wood Stock, Ltd.	840 First St.	W. Des Moines	IA
Strotman Building	625 5th N.W.	Waverly	IA

KANSAS

Unvarnished Truth	8645 Bluejacket	Lenexa	KS
Unfinished Shop	2708 W. 53rd	Shawnee Mission	KS
Timberline Unfinished Furniture	911 W. 37th St.	Topeka	KS
Jack's Furniture	708 N. Broadway	Wichita	KS

KENTUCKY

Decon's Bench	201 Court St.	Covington	KY
The Wooden Door	409 W. Main St.	Lexington	KY
Unfinished Furniture Center	4748 Bardstown Rd.	Louisville	KY
Unfinished Furniture Store	2015 Parrish Ave.	Owensboro	KY

LOUISIANA

T. L. Evans Wood Craft Furniture	2211 Richard St.	Abbeville	LA
Woodcraft Furnishings	405 Coulee Loop N.	Abbeville	LA
Sweetie's Unfinished Furniture	2927 Masonic Dr.	Alexandria	LA
Fraenkel Wholesale Furniture Co.	10600 S. Choctaw Dr.	Baton Rouge	LA
U-Finish Furniture Mart	2672 Barksdale Blvd.	Bossier City	LA
Richard's Unpainted Furniture	125 Range Ave.	Denham Springs	LA
The Wood Shoppe	419 Lapalco Blvd.	Gretna	LA
Woodworks Unfinished Furniture	118 N. Oak	Hammond	LA
Unpainted Furniture by Lou	447 Heyman Blvd.	Lafayette	LA
Andy's Unpainted Furniture Store	3239 Kirkman	Lake Charles	LA
Bare Wood Furniture	4913 Common	Lake Charles	LA
Unpainted Furniture Store	3239 Kirkman St.	Lake Charles	LA
Woodworks	4241 Veteran's Hwy.	Metairie	LA
Unfinished Furniture	2020 Metairie Rd.	Metairie	LA
Unpainted Furniture by Jackie	3217 Concordia	Monroe	LA
Nice and Easy	701 S. Lewis	New Iberia	LA
Ernst Unfinished Furniture	3242 Magazine St.	New Orleans	LA

LOUISIANA (con't.)

Furniture in the Raw	2020 Metairie Rd.	New Orleans	LA
Wood 'n Things	347 Elmira	New Orleans	LA
Marcus Furniture World	711 Milam	Shreveport	LA
Unpainted Furniture Store	1239 Shreve City Center	Shreveport	LA

MAINE

Unfinished Furniture House	Rainbow Mall	Portland	ME

MARYLAND

The Unfinished Shoppe	10525 York Rd.	Cockeysville	MD
Saah Furniture	7900 Cessna Ave.	Gaithersburg	MD

MASSACHUSETTS

University Furniture	1042 Beacon St.	Brookline	MA
Cambridge Unfinished Furniture	453 Massachusetts Ave.	Cambridge	MA
Circle Unpainted Furniture	281 Concord Ave.	Cambridge	MA
County Workshop	2327 Massachusetts Ave.	Cambridge	MA
Unfinished Furniture House	Rural Route 114	Danvers	MA
Unfinished Furniture House	650 Plymouth	East Bridgewater	MA
Unfinished Furniture House	680 Worcester Rd.	Framingham	MA
Country Home Furnishings	25 Wickman Dr.	Gardner	MA
Finishing Touch	49 Russel	Hadley	MA
Unfinished Furniture House, Inc.	Rural Route 53	Hanover	MA
Naked Furniture	237 41 Main St.	Hyannis	MA
Unfinished Furniture House	P.O. Box 200	Mansfield	MA
Gallagher Unfinished Furniture	135 Main	Medway	MA
Naked Furniture	456 Washington	Norwell	MA
Inside Out	1571 East St.	Pittsfield	MA
Pine Craft Furniture	27A Beale St.	Quincy	MA
Yankee Unfinished Furniture	Long Pd. Rd.	S. Yarmouth	MA
Jeffrey Bros., Inc.	144 Canal St.	Salem	MA
Unfinished Furniture House	College Hwy.	Southwick	MA
Unfinished Furniture House	Rural Route 27	Stoughton	MA
Unfinished Furniture House	1220 VFW Parkway	West Roxbury	MA
The Barn Door	519 Columbian	Weymouth	MA
Furniture in the Raw	857 Millbury	Worcester	MA

MICHIGAN

Jacobson Stores, Inc.	16500 Oakwood Blvd.	Allen Park	MI
Naked Furniture	3787 Washtenaw Ave. Arborland Consumer Mall	Ann Arbor	MI

MICHIGAN (con't.)

Naked Furniture	24071-75 Orchard Lake Rd.	Farmington	MI
Geppetto's Unfinished Furniture	4118 S. Saginaw	Flint	MI
Naked Furniture	3102 S. Dort Hwy.	Flint	MI
Caren's Unfinished Furniture Shoppe	921 S.W. 28th	Grand Rapids	MI
The Finishing Touch	237 E. Main	Harbor Springs	MI
Hartland House	Hartland Rd.	Hartland	MI
Naked Furniture	5140 S. Westwedge Ave.	Kalamazoo	MI
Naked Furniture	2948 28th St. S.E.	Kentwood	MI
Naked Furniture	4308 W. Saginaw	Lansing	MI
Cuttings Home Center	110 Park St.	Lapeer	MI
Finish & Save Furniture Co.	33606 Plymouth Rd.	Livonia	MI
Geppetto's Furniture	11340 N. Saginaw Rd.	Mt. Morris	MI
Wood & Wicker	316 E. Mitchell	Petoskey	MI
Naked Furniture	1038 N. Woodward	Royal Oak	MI
Wolhan Lumber Co.	1740 Midland Rd. 3400 Bay Rd.	Saginaw	MI
Naked Furniture	3570 Bay Rd.	Saginaw	MI
Naked Furniture	Riverland Shopping Ctr.	Sterling Hts.	MI
The Pinery, Inc.	1781 S. Garfield Ave.	Traverse City	MI
Donbit's Shoppe	1163-E W. Maple	Walled Lake	MI

MINNESOTA

Saw Mill Unpainted Furniture	23 W. Superior St.	Duluth	MN
Buck's Unpainted	1639 Larpenteur Ave.	Falcon Hts.	MN
Buck's Unpainted	1023 Excelsier Ave. W.	Hopkins	MN
Unfinished Furniture, Etc.	1709 Madison Ave.	Mankato	MN
Naked Furniture	1898 Beam Ave.	Maplewood	MN
The Unpainted Place, Inc.	1601 Hennepin Ave.	Minneapolis	MN
Woody's Unfinished Furniture	5011 Excelsior Blvd.	Minneapolis	MN
Buck's Unpainted	2017 Woodlyn Ave. N.	St. Paul	MN
Knock on Wood Unfinished Furniture	2325 N. Fairview Ave.	Saint Paul	MN

MISSISSIPPI

Economy Furniture Co.	330 N. Liberty St.	Canton	MS
Woody's Unfinished Furniture Shop	623 Main	Greenwood	MS
Saw Mill	Rt. 11 Hwy. 49 N.	Gulfport	MS
Unpainted Furniture Co.	4030 Metro Dr.	Jackson	MS
Shaw Manufacturing, Inc.	Okolona Industrial Pk.	Oklona	MS
The Cedar Bucket Unpainted	Highway 6 West	Oxford	MS
The Finishing Touch	1051 W. Edwards	Tunica	MS
Unpainted Furniture Center	1028 Washington	Vicksburg	MS

MISSOURI

Riverside Building Supply	120 N. King's Hwy.	Cape Giradeau	MO
Naked Furniture	9222 Watson Rd.	Crestwood	MO
The Wood Works	750 New Florissant Rd. S.	Florissant	MO
Unvarnished Truth	1527 S. Noland Rd.	Independence	MO
Unfinished Furniture Shop	1510 E. 32nd	Joplin	MO
The Wood Shed	109 E. Harrison	Kirksville	MO
The Wood Works	230 S. Meramec Sta. Rd.	Manchester	MO
The Woodshop	Rt. 4	Perryville	MO
Naked Furniture	13079 New Halls Ferry Rd.	Saint Louis	MO
Pieper's Unfinished Furniture	105 E. Jefferson	Saint Louis	MO
The Wood & Shop	5605 N. Lindberg	Saint Louis	MO
The Wood Works	8865 Ladue Rd.	Saint Louis	MO
The Wood Works	4429 Lemay Ferry Rd.	Saint Louis	MO

MONTANA

The Oak Tree	1749 Grand Ave.	Billings	MT
Mostley Oak	2825 W. Main	Bozeman	MT
The Woodshed	129 W. Main	Bozeman	MT
The Nude Nook	26 E. Silver	Butte	MT
Quality Unfinished Furniture	129 Montana Ave.	Havre	MT
Unfinished Furniture Shoppe	330 Jackson St.	Helena	MT
The Woodshed	235 Spencer	Nashua	MT

NEBRASKA

Bare Woods	213 W. Mission	Bellevue	NE
DJ's Unfinished Furniture	3939 N. 48th	Lincoln	NE
John L. Hoppe Lumber Co.	75th & Cornhusker Hwy.	Lincoln	NE
Pauley Lumber Co.	945 S. 27th St.	Lincoln	NE
Kildare Home Center	108 E. 5th	North Platte	NE
Bare Necessities	3019-21 S. 83rd Plaza	Omaha	NE

NEVADA

Jacqueline's Courtyard	918 S. Valley View Blvd.	Las Vegas	NV
Wood Gallery	3025 W. Sahara	Las Vegas	NV
Bonkers Furniture	95 E. Grove St.	Reno	NV
Normark	6750 S. Virginia St.	Reno	NV
Gruner's Fine Furnishing	846 B	Sparks	NV

NEW HAMPSHIRE

U-Finish Furniture	852 2nd	Manchester	NH
Line Lumber Co.	17 Lafayette Rd.	North Hampton	NH

NEW HAMPSHIRE (con't.)

Country Wood Unfinished Furniture	Rte. 101	Raymond Hill	NH
Sand & Stain Shoppes, Inc.	Rural Route 1	Seabrook	NH

NEW JERSEY

Gelco Woodcraft Unpainted	1121 State Hwy. No. 35	Asbury Park	NJ
Huckleberry Finn	Burlington Center	Burlington	NJ
Top-O-The Barn Ready-to-Finish	Rte. 31	Buttzville	NJ
Hanco Wood Products, Inc.	28 State Hwy. No. 10	East Hanover	NJ
Erney's Unfinished Furniture	104 Mercer Mall R1 & Q	Lawrenceville	NJ
Texas Tinkerwood	1015 Linden Hill Apts.	Lindenwold	NJ
Woodloft, Inc.	K-Mart Shpg. Cntr. Rt. 3	Moorestown	NJ
Village Pine	64 Rte. 4	Paramus	NJ
S & R Quality Unpainted Furniture	548 Pennsauken Mart	Pennsauken	NJ
Pine Craft Unfinished Furniture	869 S. Broad St.	Trenton	NJ
Derbyshires	1267 Rte. 23	Wayne	NJ
Huckleberry Finn	1400 Willowbrook Mall	Wayne	NJ
Huckleberry Finn	134 Woodbridge Center	Woodbridge	NJ

NEW MEXICO

Wayte Unfinished Furniture	N. of Alamogordo	Alamogordo	NM
Naked Furniture	1105 San Mateo N.E.	Albuquerque	NM
Unpainted Furniture Ctr., Inc.	4120 Menaul Blvd. N.E.	Albuquerque	NM
The Unfinished Furniture Store	1931 N. Grimes	Hobbs	NM
Unfinished Furniture Store	324 W. Bender Blvd.	Hobbs	NM
The Wood Bin	1410 S. Main Colony House	Roswell	NM
Art Ward's Unfinished Furniture	853 Cerrillos	Santa Fe	NM
The Knot Hole	316 N. Bullard	Silver City	NM

NEW YORK

Huckleberry Finn	116 Railroad Ave.	Albany	NY
Pa's Woodshed	119 Montgomery St.	Binghamton	NY
Arista Unpainted Furniture	2129 White Plains Rd.	Bronx	NY
Beta Unpainted Furniture	2991 3rd Ave.	Bronx	NY
Fox Lumber Co.	2114 Coyle St.	Brooklyn	NY
Joseph Zolacz Lumber Co.	1400 Bailey Ave.	Buffalo	NY
Wood Grain Unfinished Furniture	Rural Route 3	Cadyville	NY
Superior Unpainted Furniture, Inc.	8200 Main	Clarence	NY
Huckleberry Finn	Pencan Mall	Clay	NY
Ultimate Unpainted Furniture, Inc.	1938 Hempstead Trnpk.	East Meadow	NY
Naked Furniture	1945 Jericho Turnpike	East Northport	NY

NEW YORK (con't.)

Furniture-in-the-Raw	699 White Plains Rd.	Eastchester	NY
Marty's Barn Cellar	Rt. 5	Elbridge	NY
Huckleberry Finn	Dutchess Mall	Fishkill	NY
Enzoo's Nude Furniture/Custom Made	6042 Myrtle Ave.	Flushing	NY
George's Unpainted Furniture	7618 Roosevelt Ave.	Flushing	NY
Lufty's Unpainted Furniture	497 Hempstead Turnpike W.	Hempstead	NY
Norman Harvey Assoc.	55 Commerce Dr.	Hauppauge	NY
Wood Land Unfinished Furniture	3184 East Henrietta Rd.	Henrietta	NY
Hicksville Unpainted Furniture	135 N. Broadway	Hicksville	NY
Enzoo's Nude Furniture	201 Hillside Ave.	Hollis	NY
Country Living	19 Saddle Ridge Dr.	Hopewell Jct.	NY
Huckleberry Finn	Arnot Mall	Horseheads	NY
Naked Furniture	97 Old Field Rd.	Huntington	NY
Unfinished Furniture Store	206 Taughnck Blvd	Ithaca	NY
Enzoo's Nude Furniture, Inc.	20120 Hillside Ave.	Jamaica	NY
Huckleberry Finn	Oakdale Mall	Johnson City	NY
Naked Furniture	1104 Ulster Ave. Mall	Kingston	NY
Huckleberry Finn	Latham Cor. Shopping Center	Latham	NY
Beta Unpainted Furniture	2701 47th Ave.	Long Island City	NY
Olympic Unpainted Furniture	3501 Queens Blvd.	Long Island City	NY
Piro's Unpainted Furniture	4526 Greenpoint Ave.	Long Island City	NY
Naked Furniture	265-B Osbourne Rd.	Loudonville	NY
Woodpecker Shop	1009 W. Boston Post Rd.	Mamaronek	NY
Pine Shed	Rt. 20 and 174	Marcellus	NY
Fireside Unfinished Furniture	517 S. Main	N. Syracuse	NY
Huckleberry Finn	Nanuet Mall	Nanuet	NY
Ottavio's Unfinished Furniture	618 Main	New Rochelle	NY
Beta Unpainted Furniture	1519 3rd Ave.	New York	NY
Beta Unpainted Furniture	455 Park Ave.	New York	NY
Beta Unpainted Furniture	18 W. 23rd	New York	NY
Eagle Unpainted Furniture	43 W. 14th	New York	NY
Furniture-in-the-Raw, Inc.	1021 2nd Ave.	New York	NY
J.N. Unpainted Furniture, Inc.	615 9th Ave.	New York	NY
Knosos Unpainted Furniture	373 S. Park Ave.	New York	NY
Krebs Stengel	200 Lexington Ave.	New York	NY
Olympic Unpainted Furniture	845 Broadway	New York	NY
Olympic Unpainted Furniture	141 5th Ave.	New York	NY
Rodos Unpainted Furniture	215 W. 79th	New York	NY
Sand R Quality Unpainted Furniture	2139 3rd Ave.	New York	NY
Village Unpainted Furniture Co.	101 E. 14th St.	New York	NY
Huckleberry Finn	South Hills Mall	Poughkeepsie	NY

NEW YORK (con't.)

Moran's Decorating Center	3760 W. Henrietta Rd.	Rochester	NY
Naked Furniture	1516 Ridge Rd. West	Rochester	NY
Real Wood Furniture	2452 W. Henrietta Rd.	Rochester	NY
Rudnicks of Penfield, Inc.	1626 Penfield Rd.	Rochester	NY
Superior Unfinished Furniture	485 Ridge Rd. W.	Rochester	NY
Flaxman Woodworking Corp.	94 S. Longbeach Rd.	Rockville Centre	NY
Oak Tree, Ltd.	153 Main St.	Sayville	NY
Furniture-in-the-Raw	650 Central Park Ave.	Scarsdale	NY
Crossroads Unfinished Furniture	790 Richmond Ave.	Staten Island	NY
Naked Furniture	1060 Niagara Falls Blvd.	Tonawanda	NY
J. Paul's Unfinished Furniture	2137 Empire Blvd.	Webster	NY
Superior Unpainted Furniture	8200 Main St.	Williamsville	NY
Unpainted Furniture City	773 Central Park Ave.	Yonkers	NY
Huckleberry Finn	Riverside Mall	Utica	NY

NORTH CAROLINA

Good Wood Unfinished Furniture	5401 S. Boulevard	Charlotte	NC
House of Unfinished Furniture	5906 Pineville Rd.	Charlotte	NC
American Intl. Furniture	301 S. Duke St.	Durham	NC
Unfinished Furniture World	831 Elm	Fayetteville	NC
Woodcrafts & Unfinished Furniture	2508 E. Ash	Goldsboro	NC
Wooden–U–Finish	1821 13th Ave. N.	Grand Forks	NC
Unfinished Furniture World	5732 High Point Rd.	Greensboro	NC
Solid Wood/Unfinished Furniture	6402 Market St.	Wilmington	NC
Unfinished Furniture World	1814 Silas Creek Pkwy.	Winston–Salem	NC

NORTH DAKOTA

Bonawitz Unfinished Furniture	16 Broadway	Fargo	ND
Blasy's Unfinished Furniture	804 5 Ave. N.E.	Mandan	ND

OHIO

Furniture & Stuff in the Buff	508 Claremont Ave.	Ashland	OH
The Woodarama Shoppe	5056 W. Tuscarawas	Canton	OH
Woodarama Shoppe	112 Perry Dr. N.W.	Canton	OH
Wayside Workshop	111 Wilson Mills Rd.	Chardon	OH
Naked Furniture	9568 Colerain Ave.	Cincinnati	OH
Swallens, Inc.	5700 Wooster Pike	Cincinnati	OH
The Wooden Door	10800 Reading Rd.	Cincinnati	OH
Unfinished Furniture Shops	7400 Kenwood Rd.	Cincinnati	OH
Unfinished Furniture Shops	9914 Colerain Ave.	Cincinnati	OH

OHIO (con't.)

Unfinished Furniture Shops	10800 Reading Rd.	Cincinnati	OH
Forest City	10800 Brookpark Rd.	Cleveland	OH
J & J Unfinished Furniture	17709 Euclid	Cleveland	OH
Unfinished Wood Furniture Store	3403 South Blvd.	Columbus	OH
Wood Craft	7675 Old Troy Pike	Dayton	OH
Mike's Paint & Supply	1801 W. State St.	Fremont	OH
Woodcraft South	4728 Wilmington Pike	Kettering	OH
Furniture in the Nude	1540 Elida Rd.	Lima	OH
Naked Furniture	7619 Mentor Ave.	Mentor	OH
Naked Furniture	9 Prestige Plaza	Miamisburg	OH
Naked Furniture	13387 Smith Rd.	Middleburg Hts.	OH
K & G Unfinished Furniture	1600 E. Main St.	Newark	OH
Unfinished Wood Furniture Stores	4825 E. Main St.	Reynoldsburg	OH
Root 62 Enterprises	15518 Rt. 62	Salem	OH
Naked Furniture	3301 W. Central	Toledo	OH
A & B Unfinished Furniture	1445 Elm Rd. N.E.	Warren	OH

OKLAHOMA

Finishing Touch	2524 S.E. Washington Blvd.	Bartlesville	OK
Ready to Finish	6660 N.W. 39th	Bethany	OK
Jane's Finishing Touch	24 Cache Road Square	Lawton	OK
Natural Interiors	9300 S. I-35	Oklahoma City	OK
Al's Woodcraft	4316 S. Sheridan	Tulsa	OK

OREGON

Stanton Unfinished Furniture	10175 S.W. Beaverton Hwy.	Beaverton	OR
Lloyd's Redi-To-Finish Furniture	1135 N.W. Galveston	Bend	OR
Sageland Furniture	63270 Lyman Pl.	Bend	OR
The Woodtique	521 Hwy. 99 N.	Eugene	OR
Classic Woods Unfinished Furniture	2458 E. Burnside	Gresham	OR
Murphy's Unfinished Furniture	1545 S.E. TV Hwy.	Hillsboro	OR
Jones' Unfinished Furniture	421 Commercial	Klamath Falls	OR
Grantree Furniture	201 S.W. Arthur	Portland	OR
Murphy's Unfinished Furniture	804 S.W. 3rd	Portland	OR
Natural Furniture	800 N.E. Broadway	Portland	OR
The Unfinished Furniture Co.	824 N.W. Murray Rd.	Portland	OR
Union Furniture	3590 S.E. Hawthorne Blvd.	Portland	OR
Gevurtz Furniture	6600 S.W. Bonita Rd.	Tigard	OR

PENNSYLVANIA

Paint 'n Pine	5800 6th Ave.	Altoona	PA
Brookside Lumber & Supply	500 Logan Rd.	Bethel Park	PA
Knot Hole Unfinished Furniture	324 Mill	Bristol	PA
Worsley's Paint & Wallpaper	161 N. Main St.	Butler	PA
The Whistlestop	101 S. Central Ave.	Canonsburg	PA
Mooney's Unpainted Furniture	1031 Howertown Rd.	Catasauqua	PA
Mar Stans, Inc.	Rte. 202	Chaddsford	PA
Sawdust Shops of New Jersey	Rd. 2 Box 277	Chaddsford	PA
A. Fastman, Inc.	16 E. Baltimore Ave.	Clifton Hts.	PA
Unfinished Wood Products	Rural Route 3	Ebensburg	PA
Barewoods by Jan	Rte. 8	Gibsonia	PA
Pages Factory to You	652 Main St.	Johnstown	PA
Seibert Inc. Unpainted Furniture	10 Eisenhower Blvd.	Lancaster	PA
Seibert Unpainted Furniture	1939 Columbia Ave.	Lancaster	PA
Ungars Hardware, Inc.	Olympia Shopping Center	McKeesport	PA
Spencer Paint & Glass Co.	318 320 E. Washington	New Castle	PA
Buyer's Mart	207 12th St. and Pennsylvania Ave.	Pittsburgh	PA
Naked Furniture	11663 Penn Hills Dr.	Pittsburgh	PA
King's Unpainted Furniture	692 W. Schuylkill Rd.	Pottstown	PA
Evan's Unpainted Furniture	19 E. State	Quarryville	PA
David's Unpainted Furniture	Bethlehem Pike/Schoolhouse Rd.	Telford	PA
Washington Paint & Glass Co.	138 S. Main St.	Washington	PA
Wiggin's Unpainted Furniture	1301 West Chester Pike	West Chester	PA
Naked Furniture	Willow Grove Shopping Center	Willow Grove	PA

RHODE ISLAND

Unfinished Furniture House	747 Airport Rd.	Warwick	RI

SOUTH CAROLINA

Good Wood Unfinished Furniture	4825 Forest Dr.	Columbia	SC
Naked Furniture	1623 Broad River Rd.	Columbia	SC
Naked Furniture	1540 Wade Hampton Blvd.	Greenville	SC
Wood Shaper	1600 Cedar Ln.	Greenville	SC
Southern Craftsman	Golden Strip Shopping	Mauldin	SC

SOUTH DAKOTA

World of Wood, Inc.	613 St. Joe St.	Rapid City	SD
McCaslin's Unfinished Furniture	2601 W. 41st	Sioux Falls	SD

TENNESSEE

Unpainted Furniture Co.	2404 Gallatin Rd. N.	Goodlettsville	TN
The Wood Shed	College Square Shopping Center	Harriman	TN

TENNESSEE (con't.)

Unpainted Furniture World	Hollywood Shopping Center	Jackson	TN
Unpainted Furniture of Knoxville	7219 Kingston Pke.	Knoxville	TN
Raw Furniture Shoppe, Ltd.	5353 Mendenhall Mall	Memphis	TN
Raw Furniture Shoppe, Ltd.	5254 Summer Ave.	Memphis	TN
Unpainted Furniture Center	3526 Jackson Ave.	Memphis	TN
Unpainted Furniture Center	4100 S. Plaza Dr.	Memphis	TN
Ready-To-Finish Furniture	2301 S. 12th Ave.	Nashville	TN
The Wood Shoppe	178 Randolph Rd.	Oak Ridge	TN

TEXAS

Imiwac	4003 S. Hwy. 288	Angleton	TX
The Wood Shed	2833 Galleria Dr.	Arlington	TX
Furniture in the Raw	7713 Burnet Rd.	Austin	TX
Naked Furniture of Austin	5501 N. Lamar Suite B	Austin	TX
Unpainted Furniture Centers	5329 N. IH 35	Austin	TX
Shay's	Rt. 3	Baytown	TX
Sawmill	Gaylynn Center	Beaumont	TX
The Wood Shed	315 N. Washington	Beeville	TX
Woodbin Corp.	1110 W. Beltline	Carrollton	TX
Furniture in the Raw	3902 S. Padres Isle Dr.	Corpus Christi	TX
Naked Furniture	2505 Mimosa St.	Corsicana	TX
The Wood Works	13362 Preston Rd.	Dallas	TX
Tinkerwood	Valley View Center	Dallas	TX
Unpainted Furniture	10149 Trail Pine	Dallas	TX
Nude Furniture	6700 Camp Bowie Blvd.	Forth Worth	TX
The Unfinished Furniture Store	5059 Old Grandbury Rd.	Forth Worth	TX
The Wood Shed	6978 Green Oaks Rd.	Forth Worth	TX
The Wood Shed	8755 Bedford-Euless Rd.	Forth Worth	TX
The Finishing Touch	126 S. Friendswood Dr.	Friendswood	TX
Tinkerwood	1184 Baybrook Mall	Friendswood	TX
Neusch Bros. Nude Furnitureware	1616 N. Dixon	Gainesville	TX
Furniture in the Raw	973 W. Centerville	Garland	TX
Furniture in the Raw	8412 S. Gessner	Houston	TX
Houston Unfinished Furniture	724 W. FM 1960	Houston	TX
Houston Unpainted Furniture	1640 W. FM 1960	Houston	TX
Nude Furniture	1809 N. Gessner	Houston	TX
U-Semble It Furniture Store	3202 Fondren	Houston	TX
Unpainted Furniture Distributors	4660 Pine Timbers	Houston	TX
House of Woods	1007 E. Irving Blvd.	Irving	TX

TEXAS (con't.)

Naked Furniture	2533 Judson Rd. North Loop	Longview	TX
Two by Four	2520 34th	Lubbock	TX
P.J.'s Unfinished Furniture Center	609 W. Hwy. 83	McAllen	TX
Unpainted Furniture Store	16 Imperial Shopping	Midland	TX
Bald Furniture	8505 Gulf Fwy.	Pasadena	TX
Neal's Unfinished Furniture	3100 Independence Pkwy.	Plano	TX
Furniture in the Raw	1552 Babcock	San Antonio	TX
Furniture in the Raw	2347 N.W. Military Hwy.	San Antonio	TX
Vilage Woodcrafter	703 Serenade	San Antonio	TX
Unpainted Furniture	218 E. Kingbury	Seguin	TX
Unfinished Furniture Villa	5631 Hwy. 75	Sherman	TX
Freeman's Unpainted Furniture Center	1808 W. 7th	Texarkana	TX
Woodshed	3601 S. Broadway	Tyler	TX
Woodstock Unpainted Furniture	3324 Franklin Ave.	Waco	TX
Finishing Touch	2605 Seymour Hwy.	Wichita Falls	TX
Furniture Buff	3608 Call Field Rd.	Wichita Falls	TX

UTAH

Naked Furniture	6885 S. State	Midvale City	UT
U-Finish Wood Furniture	1150 W. Riverdale Rd.	Ogden	UT
Natural Wood Furniture	1100 E. Cedar Ave.	Provo	UT
Ready-To-Finish Furniture	3333 S. State	Salt Lake City	UT
Wood House	412 South 700 W.	Salt Lake City	UT
Oak'n Decor	9976 S. 22430 E.	Sandy	UT
The Woodworks	9200 S. 700 E.	Sandy	UT

VERMONT

The Woodshed Unfinished Furniture	50 Prospect	Barre	VT
Sam's Unfinished Furntiure	372 N. Winooski Ave.	Burlington	VT
Coventry Country Store	Main St.	Coventry	VT
King's Unfinished Furniture	31 Main	Fair Haven	VT

VIRGINIA

Saah Bookcase	2330 Columbia Pike	Arlington	VA
Naked Furniture	9408A Main St. Pickett Shopping Center	Fairfax	VA
Zug's Unfinished Furniture	115 E. Loudoun St.	Leesburg	VA
The Wooden Chair	5218 Fort Ave.	Lynchburg	VA

VIRGINIA (cont.)

Unpainted Furniture Store	1201 Mall Dr.	Midlothian	VA
Unpainted Furniture Store	23 Southern Shopping Center	Norfolk	VA
Rawles Aden Lumber Co.	River St.	Petersburg	VA
Unpainted Furniture	1201 Mall Dr.	Richmond	VA
Woodmaster	4119 Brandon Ave.	Roanoke	VA
Beahm's Woodshed	5905 Noblestown Rd. #D	Springfield	VA

WASHINGTON

Bellevue Unfinished Furniture	Crossroads Shopping Center	Bellevue	WA
Oak Reflections	106 S.E. 102nd	Bellevue	WA
Worldwide Woods Unfinished Furniture	305 Callow N.	Bremerton	WA
The Unfinished Store	1348 Old Hwy. 99	Burlington	WA
Bare Wood Furniture	110 Harrison	Centralia	WA
Snyder's U-Finish Wood Furniture	284 N. Main	Colville	WA
Worldwide Woods, Inc.	12057 124th Ave. N.E.	Kirkland	WA
Western House of Wood	1015 15th Ave.	Longview	WA
Plaza Unfinished Furniture	470 North Bend Way	North Bend	WA
The Furniture Factory	9026 900th Ave W.	Oak Harbor	WA
The Woodshed Unfinished Furniture	3663 Pacific Ave.	Olympia	WA
The Unfinished Furniture Store	10712 112th E.	Puyallup	WA
Towne Unfinished Furniture	16300 Redmond Way	Redmond	WA
B & D Unfinished Furniture	826 S. 3rd	Renton	WA
A–America, Inc.	18405 72nd Ave. S.	Seattle	WA
B & D Unfinished Furniture	4449 35th S.W.	Seattle	WA
Ballard Unfinished Furniture	1712 N.W. Market St.	Seattle	WA
Bare Chest	5506 35th N.E.	Seattle	WA
Don Willis Furniture	10516 Lake City Way	Seattle	WA
Underhills Unfinished Furniture	17034 Aurora Ave. N.	Seattle	WA
Walker's Unfinished Furniture	N. 1622 Division	Spokane	WA
Fridays Unfinished Furniture	9201 Pacific Ave.	Tacoma	WA
Unfinished Furniture Center	3730 S. Pine	Tacoma	WA
Real Furniture	208 W. Main	Walla Walla	WA
Wood 'n Things	240 N. Wenatchee Ave.	Wenatchee	WA
Artcraft	1406 S. 1st St.	Yakima	WA

WEST VIRGINIA

Contemporary Gallery	3806 MacCorkle Ave.	Charleston	WV
Nature's Furniture, Inc.	203 Virginia St. W.	Charleston	WV
Riter Furniture Co.	1921 Third Ave.	Huntington	WV

WISCONSIN

Unfinished Business	430 W. College Ave.	Appleton	WI
Unfinished Business	305 S. Bartstown	Euclaire	WI
Westphal's Hardware	2030 E. Mason St.	Green Bay	WI
Wood World	1214 S. Military Ave.	Green Bay	WI
Wooden Goods	1270 Main	Green Bay	WI
Naked Furniture	5495 S. 76th St.	Greendale	WI
Carver's Bench, Inc.	1452 Sheridan Rd.	Kenosha	WI
Naked Furniture	6017 Odana Rd.	Madison	WI
A–1 Unpainted Furniture Mart	2323 E. Washington Ave.	Madison	WI
Unpainted Furniture Co.	10633 W. Oklahoma Ave.	Milwaukee	WI
Naked Furniture	6100 W. Washington	Racine	WI
Wood Pile	209 S. 4th St.	River Falls	WI
Naked Furniture	109 E. Silverspring Dr.	Whitefish Bay	WI

HOW TO FINISH READY-TO-FINISH FURNITURE

TAKING THE WITCHCRAFT OUT OF FINISHING FURNITURE

THIS CHAPTER HAS NOTHING whatever to do with finishing furniture under a full moon with a potion of bat hair and possum oil. Nor has it to do with the uttering of mystic incantations religiously preserved from the ancient rites of your forefathers in order to get a good finish.

It's incredible how God-fearing people, mostly friends and relatives, embrace mysticism when it comes to suggesting finishing techniques, especially when they have little down-to-earth experience.

Therefore, the first thing you must do is hide the fact that you are about to finish furniture from your friends and relatives.

Figure 6-1.

In other words, don't tell ol' uncle Joe you've got a finishing project unless you've got a few hours to waste while he drudges up dusty tales of how in '38 he refinished Aunt Bertha's bureau and so on, and so on. Unless you can palm off the job on him, treat the "old hand" at finishing as someone with a communicable disease.

Figure 6-2. Beware the "old hand" at finishing.

Figure 6-3. The example: A simple pine night stand. Nothing exotic or expensive ($59)—but it will show that even an inexpensive ready-to-finish item like this can be finished to rival a much more expensive piece and be a source of pride for its finisher as well.

I learned that lesson the hard way. In 1960 I was about to finish a wood chess board when a relative who shall remain anonymous suggested that instead of "store-bought" varnish I use a poultice he concocted of linseed oil. I knew I was in trouble after a week when the finish was still wet. A year later it was still tacky! And to this day—24 years later—wherever that chess board is, I'll bet a can of polyurethane that it still hasn't dried.

What this chapter will do is provide you with how I think you should finish ready-to-finish furniture.

But I owe you some clarification. This chapter is not meant for everybody. For instance, if you are passionately in love with wood to the point where you want to spend all your waking hours pampering every nook and cranny of every piece of furniture—the padded room is just down the hall. My town library features some 25 books on finishing wood, so if you're looking for an encyclopedic study on the subject, I'll lend you my library card.

This chapter is for you if you want to spend a "reasonable" amount of time to achieve a good-looking, durable finish. The majority of ready-to-finish customers, and probably you, too, fit into this group.

MY PLACE OR YOURS? THE IMPORTANCE OF PICKING A PLACE TO DO THE JOB

If you are lucky, your nearby ready-to-finish furniture store will provide you with a small area in which to finish your purchase. More stores than ever are providing space to do this to accommodate customers who lack room at home. Just ask. If your home has hardly enough room to stack the bills, plead for space with the store people before you make your purchase. Few store owners are hard-hearted enough to turn away business in the face of such a reasonable demand.

Figure 6-4. If you have a choice, do your project at the store. You'll get lots of expert advice and you don't have to clean up after.

If you do the job at home, simply choose a room, garage, basement, et cetera, with adequate ventilation. Get the air moving, preferably from inside to outside. Nothing is worse than the odor of stain saturating your new drapes for the next two months. But wait—I'll take that back. Some people stain furniture in their kitchen. What can be worse than eating potato chips tasting like Danish oil?

The next step is to stain-proof your room. That means get everything well away from the action. If your favorite lamp shade is 15 feet from where you're staining, you can be certain that some flicks of stain will have a range of 16 feet. Let Murphy's Law guide you.

A good idea to protect your floor is to open the carton that the furniture came in and use it for a floor covering. The inner layer of cardboard will absorb most stains. If you tip over the can, however, please do not send me the bill for new carpeting.

Now that you've protected your workplace it's a good idea to protect yourself. Most finishing materials are flammable. And so is your house. Make it a rule to dispose of all paper towels, rags, tack cloths, and so forth as soon as you finish using them.

The rule about proper ventilation goes beyond protecting your furnishings from lingering odors. Breathing finishing materials for a long time in a confined space can get you squirrelly. I have no idea what it actually does to your lungs in the relatively short time you use it at home, but why take chances? I like you, and I worry about you. After all, you bought my book, didn't you? So use a lot of ventilation.

TOOLS YOU'LL NEED

The following is an outline of steps and procedures involved in finishing an item of furniture:

1. Inspection
2. Sanding
3. Inspection
4. Oil Stain or Danish Oil
5. Final Finish
   a. Nothing
   b. Wax
   c. Tung Oil
   d. Tung Oil Varnish
   e. Polyurethane

Figure 6-5. For a good, satisfying finish, you'll need a tack cloth, paper towels, poly brushes, sandpaper, and steel wool.

Inspection

It should go without saying that to have a good wood finish you must start with a good hunk of wood. However, the most important time to inspect that piece of ready-to-finish furniture is *before* you get it home. Ask to open the box at the store for inspection. Make sure there are no obvious scratches, shipping damages, and other types of injury to the wood. These days most furniture is cartoned properly with the appropriate inner packing, but it's also true that some isn't. In fact, some furniture is shipped "blanket-wrapped"—without any cartoning. Getting rid of small scratches and gouges is tough enough when you're ready to finish a piece, so try to get a reasonably "clean" piece with which to start.

The second inspection should be at home before you even think about sanding the piece. Place a bright light nearby and bend down to view the wood surfaces in the reflected light. This will show up even tiny scratches. Next, run your hand over all the outer surfaces to determine which areas need the most attention. Finally, feel around the *under-surfaces*. The *under-surfaces* can best be defined as anywhere picky Aunt Bertha can get a white glove.

For a proper job, anywhere you can reach should feel smooth and comfortable. Nothing is as disturbing as snagging your polyester pants on a rough surface under a dining table you finished yourself. Worse yet, it may happen to a dinner guest. So prepare to smooth not only what you see but what you can reach as well.

Watch Out for Glue

As you are inspecting for rough spots to sand, be on the lookout for any glue spatters on the wood. Glue will resist taking the color of any stain. If you stain over spatters of glue you will be left with splatters of white spots. Inspect in areas where spindles fit into the seat of a chair, for instance.

Another place to look for glue spots is around any exposed joint. There is more on how to remove glue later.

By doing a detailed inspection at home before you start working, you accomplish more than just planning your sanding. You will catch hidden damages that you may not have seen during your in-store inspection. This is also the best time to get service on damages from the store—well within the allowable time you have to return merchandise.

Take It Apart

This is probably the best time to cover the benefits of disassembly before you start to sand a piece. Take out all the unattached shelves, remove doors and drawers, and remove glass from its frame if possible. In short, take as much apart as you feel confident you can get back together again. This will allow you to work on these items in a convenient place and in a comfortable position, rather than have to bend down and stick your head inside of something.

Figure 6-6. If you can get it back together, take it apart.

SANDING

I suppose that there is someone somewhere out there who hasn't used sandpaper before, so we'll get down to the basics of what sandpaper to use and how to use it.

For ready-to-finish furniture you'll usually need three grades of sandpaper:

Grit size #220—to use before you stain

Grit size #400—to use between finishing coats

Grit size #600—to use before final finish coat

Since not all professional finishers agree on the kind of sandpaper to use, I will go out on a limb and say that whatever brand is recommended in a ready-to-finish specialty store will be fine. Most stores will carry a "garnet" or an "aluminum oxide" type.

If you plan to finish some very low-priced furniture that feels fairly rough to the touch, ask for a sheet or two of grit size #150. It will cut faster and easier than the #220 size.

About Steel Wool

I hate steel wool. It feels terrible to the touch and all those little steel bits fall off and get all over. But when you need to smooth chair spindles, carved legs, and other irregular surfaces, however, steel wool works great. It is also the best way to get into the corners of bookcases and other hard to reach places. Ask for steel wool grade 2/0 or 3/0. If you will be buying some of the more expensive furniture items, you may also want to buy some 4/0 steel wool, as very little smoothing will be needed.

HOW TO SAND

Sanding is the mechanical scratching off of the topmost wood surface. Since it is a scratching action, if you sand with the direction of the grain, the scratching won't show as much. So the first rule of sanding is: *always sand with the grain.*

If you're lazy like me, an electric sander may be used. If it's a vibrating sander or a finishing sander, you're home free. But don't think you can use a belt sander or a disk sander to finish furniture—all you'll get is a pile of sawdust.

Figure 6-7. An electric sander like this pays for itself the first hour.

If you don't have an electric sander the easiest way to sand by hand is to make a sanding block. Just wrap the sandpaper around a block of wood. This makes an easy-to-grip tool that makes for a nice flat surface.

Most ready-to-finish furniture is pre-sanded at the factory. When you are at the store take some time to feel several items. Some will feel slightly coarse to the touch. That is the furniture you'll start sanding with the #220 grit sandpaper. Some of the higher-priced furniture items will feel so smooth that you won't see any

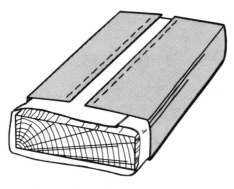

Figure 6-8. Fold up an old piece of sandpaper or several layers of paper towels as a pad under the block.

point to sanding them any more. These items should be gone over lightly before you stain with a very fine 4/0 steel wool to remove finger prints, scuff marks—in short, anything that may resist the oil stain from penetrating into the wood.

The person who wants to do a very conscientious finishing job will carry the sanding much farther. This includes sanding the surfaces *inside* the piece as well; so a coat of clear finish or stain can be used on the inside wood surfaces to protect against mildew and dampness.

Figure 6-9. Sanding the inside makes a coat of finish go farther to protect against dampness.

Can You Sand Too Much?

Yes! If you plan to use a medium or dark stain on a hardwood piece, it is possible to sand too much. The objective is to get as smooth a surface as possible without "polishing" it to such a degree of slickness that stain will have a tough time penetrating. On many hardwoods polishing is a danger if you go much finer than a #220 sandpaper.

Don't Forget the Tack Cloth

The tack cloth is used to remove all the sawdust and steel wool filings from the wood before you stain. It's a tacky cloth that grabs up everything that shouldn't be there. Sure, you can use a vacuum or even blow off the sawdust with your mouth. But even after all that there still will be a lot of sawdust on the surface. Invest the dollar or so for a tack cloth and you won't worry about getting little bits of garbage in your final finish ever again. I promise.

Last Inspection

Now that you've sanded or steel-wooled your furniture it's time for final inspection. Look again at the surfaces in reflected light. Any scratches, however tiny, will show up immediately when you apply the stain. That's because the wood fibers in scratches are broken and absorb much more stain into the scratch.

Let's say you do see a small scratch on a very visible area that your careful sanding did not remove. Wait! Don't sand just that scratch—you'll cause a valley in the wood. You'll sand out the scratch, but leave a "hole."

Take a moist sponge or paper towel and dab water into the scratch. This will cause the wood fibers to expand and fill the scratch mark. Wait until the spot is dry, or you can dry the area quickly with a hair dryer on a cool setting.

If you had to moisten a large area to treat the scratch, moisten the entire top. Then, after drying, carefully resand the whole top equally. If the scratch is in a veneer top, and not too deep, use the same technique but be very careful not to sand through the veneer.

Figure 6-10. This unstained board has an s-shaped scratch from the top to the bottom. Can you see it?

Figure 6-11. After staining, the scratch is obvious, especially on the softer woods. On this wood sample board, the second band from the top is oak, which is very resistant to scratches.

BID ADIEU TO GLUE

Figure 6-12 a. and b. Glue spatters before and after staining.

a

b

In the last few years glue spots have become much less of a problem with ready-to-finish furniture due to better quality control by the manufacturers. However, nothing so surprises and frustrates finishers—especially first-time finishers—than to see mysterious white spots on their newly stained piece.

Now's the time to get rid of any glue spatters that are on the wood. Use a razor blade or a sharp knife that you can lay flat on the surface of the wood next to the glue. Slide the blade in the direction of the grain of the wood and shave off the raised part of the glue (Figure 6-13). Many times the spot of glue will "pop" off. If there is some glue remaining, hold the blade upright like a brush and use a scraping motion. The glue will come off like a fine powder. If you take care not to scratch too much under the surface of the wood, it will be a simple matter to resand lightly over that spot and have the stain absorb normally.

Figure 6-13. Make sure you slide blade with the grain.

Figure 6-14 a. and b. Use a very light brushing motion, then sand.

a

b

Many times, though, the glue will be invisible until you apply the first coat of stain. It will show up as very visible white areas. To fix these, have a sharp blade handy to gently scrape the wood as described above. Then sand carefully and reapply the stain. This will cure most glue spots.

If the glue spot still resists stain, there is a little trick that works if the area is small. Scrape up some of the pigment that settled on the bottom of the can and use it as a "paint." Dab it on the spot and allow it to remain there for an hour or more. This will allow that spot additional time to absorb stain. The pigment that does not absorb into the wood dries on top of the wood and covers the spot, much like a paint.

Don't Fill Those Holes!

If there are visible nail holes or any other small areas that you would like to fill with wood patch, *do not* do so now. It's best to stain the area first with the wood stain you've chosen for the piece, then apply a wood patch that matches the color of your stain. Although the makers of wood patch say that their patch absorbs any stain, it does so differently than the wood.

Most ready-to-finish items that have exposed nail holes are very easy to work with. Simply make sure, using a nail set, that the nails are beneath the surface of the wood. Then, after proper sanding, stain the piece as usual. Often, the nail holes that seemed so obvious practically disappear. The liquid stain causes the wood fibers surrounding the nail holes to expand, nearly covering the hole.

Before You Stain, Treat the End Grain

The end grain is where the wood is cut off across the grain, exposing the long, straw-like wood fibers. End grain loves stain! It can't get enough to drink.

When you apply stain to end grain it is absorbed very quickly, causing a darker color than

Figure 6-15. Here are two examples of end grain: the routed ends of the tops and the drawer fronts.

the other wood areas. What you are left with is a very dark, perhaps black, end grain. Even though you may be using, say, a medium or light brown stain, most of the brown color will be lost.

If you want to prevent this there are two simple ways to go. The traditional method is to cover the end grain with a very light coat of shellac. This will seal off much of the end grain's ability to absorb stain. Then stain the whole piece. If the stain is not looking dark enough on the end grain simply sand off part of the shellac and restain.

If you're like me, however, you probably don't have shellac around, so in the interest of making your life easier there is another little trick. Since you are probably going to use polyurethane on the project anyway, simply dip a clean poly brush into the polyurethane and apply a thin coat to the end grain. Then wait five minutes before you stain the area. The poly will resist the stain somewhat by clogging up much of the end grain fibers. The brown tone will be

preserved. If you allow the polyurethane to dry too much before you apply the stain, or if you get some polyurethane slopping over onto the other wood areas, you can always sand it off, then re-apply the poly to the end grain, and re-stain.

Figure 6-16. Sand end grain well, then apply polyurethane carefully.

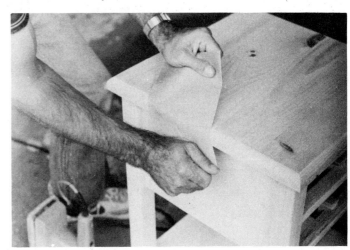

STAINING

At last, the fun part! But first, what kind of stain should you use? There are all kinds of stains: pigmented oil wiping stains, penetrating oil stains, water stains, alcohol stains, paste and jelly stains, non-grain raising stains, varnish stains, and padding stains. All of these have certain advantages and disadvantages. But I won't even begin to describe the details of all these types because you really need only to know about the two kinds of stains that are the best for ready-to-finish furniture: pigmented oil wiping stains and penetrating oil stains.

Pigmented Oil Wiping Stains

These are the most popular stains for home use. For years they have been the stain of choice for ready-to-finish furniture dealers. They are made of finely ground color pigments suspended in an oil solution. This is as close to a "foolproof" stain as possible. It can be applied with anything handy—you can even pour it onto the piece. If you put on too much, you simply wipe it off, no harm done.

Figure 6-17. These are a few of the many top national brands of quality pigmented oil wiping stains.

In general, the faster you wipe it off, the lighter the color will be; the longer you leave it on, the darker the color will be. So you have more control over the color with this type of stain than with any other type.

These stains are especially suited for pine and the softer, small-pore hardwoods such as birch, ash, aspen, and cottonwood. On open-pore woods such as oak, the pigment particles tend to clog up in the pores, showing up as a cloudy appearance. Admittedly, this is a very minor effect easily overlooked by most finishers.

About the only other drawback to these types of stains is that they have to be stirred frequently because the pigments like to settle on the bottom of the can, especially when the can has been sitting unused for some time.

A word of caution: Beware of non-national brands of stain that are often sold in some discount stores. I've seen some that have been little more than a can of muddy ink. Stick to the national brands or brands carried by ready-to-finish furniture stores.

Penetrating Oil Stains

These are also called Danish oils and are recommended by nearly every ready-to-finish dealer because it's easy to get a smooth, even color with little work or experience. These stains have no solid pigments (they are dissolved into a synthetic or natural oil-based liquid) so they penetrate deeply and allow the natural beauty of the wood to show through.

Danish oils are also considered a true *finish* because they soak into the pores of the wood and fill the wood cells with a synthetic material that hardens as it dries. Because of this hardening effect on the surface wood cells, the penetrating oil stains can be considered a one-step finish, requiring no other clear coating.

One drawback is that penetrating oils soak in faster than the pigmented wiping oil stains, so they do not offer as much control over the color intensity.

In general, use a pigmented oil wiping stain for any wood, although with an open-pore

Figure 6-18. Some of the leading Danish oils.

wood such as oak I would recommend the Danish oils as slightly preferable. For the more natural look, choose the Danish oils without any other finish.

HOW TO APPLY STAIN

The first step to proper application of stain is to use the right color stain to begin with. *This means that you must test the stain on an out-of-*

the-way place. Sample boards at the store are only approximations of what the color will look like on your furniture. Assume that the wood on your furniture is going to be cut differently than the sample boards. So never—repeat, never—start staining without testing the stain from that particular can on wood from your particular piece of furniture.

Test That Stain

A good test area that is out of sight is the side of a drawer. Just make sure that you sand the test area in the same manner as the rest of the piece. An area that is rough will almost always come out too dark. The color of the wet stain on the wood will be very close to the final color after the finish is dry and the job complete.

If the side of the drawer is not the same wood as the rest of the piece, try the inside front of the drawer.

It is rare that the color will vary between two cans of the same color stain you purchase, but if it's a pigmented oil wiping stain—the kind that often gets a gloppy pigment accumulation on the bottom of the can—make sure that you stir the new can as well as the first in order to match the color. Better yet, if you think that you'll need to open another can be-

Figure 6-19. Sand the test area well.

How Much Stain and Finish You'll Need

	STAINS		FINISHES	
	Oil Stain	Danish Oil	Tung Oil	Polyurethane
1 chair/rocker	½ pt.	½ pt.	½ pt.	½ pt.
5-drawer chest	1 pt.	1 pt.	1 pt.	1 pt.
Large dining table	1 pt.	1 pt.	1 pt.	1 pt.
Large bookcase	1–2 pts.	1–2 pts.	1 pt.	1–2 pts.

fore the job is done, open it early and mix the two cans together.

Only after you are satisfied that you've done all the sanding that is necessary (and after you have tested the stain) is it time to apply stain on the rest of the piece.

Wipe It On

How you get the stain onto the wood is up to you. If you don't like to get your hands dirty, use a poly brush.

Another way to get the job done quickly is to simply dunk a paper towel into the can and slosh it all over the piece. As you cover the wood you'll notice areas that will require more stain and areas that don't seem to drink up so much. About the only mistake you can make at this point is not to put enough stain on.

There are some differences among brands as to how long you must leave the stain on before you wipe off the excess. Some say fifteen minutes; some say ten. It's safe to assume that you're okay if you wipe it off before it starts getting tacky and tough to wipe off. Read the label on the can before you start.

If you are using a Danish oil stain, you will probably be asked to wipe off the stain with the

Figure 6-20. A poly brush works great for staining.

same rag with which you applied it. This is to assure that you will not take off too much oil too quickly. Danish oils dry somewhat sooner, and, as I said before, about the only way you can make a mistake is by putting on too little stain.

Some Danish oil makers recommend that you wipe on their oil with fine steel wool. I've never liked that method because I don't like steel wool much, and I've always found that applying Danish oil with a poly brush works just as well.

There are some other suggested methods to wipe on the stain. Some say to wipe it on first across the grain, then with the grain. I've tried it that way, but as far as I can tell it doesn't make much difference. As long as you stroke the stain with the direction of the grain before it begins to dry, you will not be bothered by any streaking across the grain.

Work Flat

It makes staining easier if you always apply the stain to a horizontal surface. Just tip the piece over so that the side you're staining is on top. If you must apply stain to a vertical surface, apply from the bottom up so you don't get a lot of drips to blend in.

Wipe It Off

I like to use paper towels to wipe off the excess stain as well as to apply the stain. Maybe it's because I know that I'll throw them away right after I'm done with them, and they won't be lying around stinking up the place. If you're a rag kind of person, so be it. Just remember to get rid of those rags quickly to minimize any fire risk.

Second Coat

After your stain is wiped off, you need to wait from 12 to 24 hours before applying the second coat. Why a second coat? Wait around a few hours and look at the first coat of stain. As it

dries it will fade rapidly. The second coat seems to lock in more of the color.

How long you wait until you apply the second coat will vary with each brand's instructions. Old-timers swear that you must wait until the first coat is bone dry before you apply the second coat, but as a practical rule I've often applied the second coat as soon as the first coat looks like it's fading. On a low-humidity day this fading can occur after two or three hours. I'm not recommending this shortcut to those who feel that this might diminish the rich look of that color stain, but I've never felt that I've lost anything by it.

The most important waiting time that you won't want to fool around with is the time after your second coat of stain and the first coat of polyurethane. Wait at least 24 hours, but more if it's very humid where you're doing the job. This is because some polyurethanes can cause the stain color to bleed if it's not dry, thus causing a cloudy-looking finish.

FINAL FINISHES

Now you're ready for the icing on the cake. What will you use to give your furniture the lasting protection it deserves? As few as ten years ago your choices would be limited, indeed. You'd be saddled with varnish or shellac unless you had the experience needed to use lacquer. Today, you have several superb finishes to choose from—all of which are easily used by the occasional finisher. Let's look at two non-choices first, and then three finishes that I can heartily recommend.

Nothing

As strange as it may seem, about three out of every 100 ready-to-finish pieces are never finished. Most of these seem to be the inexpensive chest purchased for the garage or for inside someone's closet. While this is definitely not a recommended finish—or non-finish if you like—there is no harm done to the piece if you just use it, period. About all that will happen is that it will get dirty looking. So, if you just need something to hold tools in the basement, or fabric in the back closet, no one need know your secret.

Wax

This is a finish, I guess, but I've never been one to invest time in a project just in order to be awarded the benefit of doing it again every few months. I would not recommend a wax finish for anyone but the most idle.

Tung Oil

Now we're starting to talk finishes. The public has rediscovered tung oil recently, probably because people want a "natural-looking" finish. Tung oil comes from the nut of the tung tree. They say that tung oil was used as a preserving agent in the Great Wall of China. Well, if it's good enough for the Great Wall, is it good enough for something as mundane as furniture? You bet.

Tung oil is probably the easiest finish to apply. It's so easy, in fact, I won't even bother to illustrate the steps.

Simply wipe it on until the entire surface is covered—then immediately wipe off all the excess. Keep looking for wet spots and wipe dry right away. (Note: there are some tung oil manufacturers who recommend that you wipe the oil on with your *hand*. I've tried that and all I got was a smelly hand. Next time it went on with a poly brush!)

You can put on as many coats of tung oil as you like as long as you buff with fine steel wool between well-dried coats. The final coat will be resistant to water and alcohol.

Tung Oil Varnish

This is applied much like the tung oil above, but will form more of a coating on the top of the wood. The first coat will give a satin finish. Additional coats will be glossy. It's an ideal final finish for those wipe-on addicts who abhor even the thought of applying of finish with a brush.

Polyurethane

This is the supreme finish for the do-it-yourselfer. Polyurethane is the toughest, most water- and heat-resistant final finish for furniture. It takes a bit more care to apply than the tung oils or tung oil varnishes, but it builds up on the wood quicker to provide a thick coating in a surprisingly short time. When any furni-

Figure 6-21. Both kinds of tung oil work great.

Figure 6-22. Some of the leading brands of polyurethane.

ture item is expected to undergo rough use, such as a bartop, kitchen table, or dresser top, you'll want polyurethane. If you are finishing furniture on which kids will climb, jump, or commit other such mayhem, polyurethane is a must.

The only tough choice you have to make with polyurethane is whether you want a glossy finish or a satin one. For furniture, a satin finish is preferred by do-it-yourselfers ten to one.

APPLYING POLYURETHANE

No Dust

Polyurethane and dust do not mix well. The first coat, however, is not as hateful toward dust as the last coat. So if you workplace tends toward the dusty, consider moving the piece elsewhere for the last coat.

Work Level

As with staining, a flat, level piece is easiest to work on. You'll be more comfortable, but more important, you'll get fewer runs and sags.

No Brushes, Please

I know, the old-timers will wince when I say this, but you don't need a brush to apply polyurethane. I've gone through my share of $20 brushes and every last one of them dropped a bristle or more into the final coat. The thing to use is a poly brush, or more correctly named, a poly applicator. It's simply a sponge-like applicator that absorbs polyurethane and lays it down as nice as can be without shedding bristles. And even more appealing is the fact that you don't ever clean it—you throw it away. And they're cheap—for a few dollars you can buy enough poly brushes for the entire job.

Apply First Coat

Open the can and stir the polyurethane slowly. (Never shake it! Shaking causes bubbles.) Dip the poly brush into the can, and gently tap the brush against the inside of the can. Do not drag the brush over the can's edge because that can cause tiny bubbles.

Brush on the poly by laying it on, with the grain, in one long stroke from one end of the surface to the other. If that's too long a distance, lift up the brush about halfway and make another pass from the opposite end, making sure that the two strokes are well blended in the middle.

As you finish applying the first coat, inspect the coverage carefully. If you see any lap marks or areas where there is too much poly, carefully smooth them out with the tip of the poly brush. Note any problems you see, so that you can correct your technique during the next coat.

When you're finished with the first coat, try to stay out of that room until the next day. Most of the polyurethane makers recommend at least a 24-hour drying time before applying the next coat. If the air is humid, figure about twice as long. Many of the instructions will also give a *maximum* time to elapse before the next coat. That's because if you wait too long, the finish cures to such a hard degree, you'd have to sand thoroughly in order for the next coat to "stick."

When the first coat is dry, it's time to sand with the #400 wet/dry paper. The technique to use for wet-sanding is simple. Sponge water onto the surface. What you want to do is sand off the tiny specks of roughness without removing the smooth areas. So don't *sand* like you do on raw wood. With #400 sandpaper, *lightly* draw the sandpaper along the direction of the grain, keeping it very flat with minimum pressure. Then feel the area. It should be very smooth to the touch. Go over each area until it feels smooth. (Important note: If the surface seems tacky when you start sanding, stop. You must wait several more hours—perhaps a full day for complete dryness.)

As you sand pay special attention to any rough spots, but make sure you go over every square inch. This is the time to make sure you sand out all runs, sags, and any other excess buildup. Be especially careful not to sand off the first coat. This can easily occur along the edges.

For an even smoother finish, you can graduate from the #400 to the #600 wet/dry sandpaper.

Next, wipe off all moist residue with a paper towel. When the surface is dry, go over every part with a tack cloth so that there is no chance that any tiny flecks will affect the second and/or final coat.

Figure 6-23.

Shortcut Inspection

Inspect the piece carefully. Do you really need a second coat? If you have a nice smooth surface with ample coverage of polyurethane, and the piece will not be subject to heavy use, you've probably done enough. If you want a "deeper" look that two coats will give you, you're ready for the next step.

Apply the Second Coat

For most uses this will also be your last coat. The best-quality polyurethanes have enough solids to provide an ample build-up usually after one coat, with two coats offering maximum protection. If you're coating pine, however, much more will be absorbed into the wood and you probably should use a second coat.

I know that you'll want to use a poly brush again; just make sure that it's a clean new one.

Now apply the second coat as you did the first coat, but with one important exception. You will not have to apply nearly as much polyurethane with each stroke. Let it flow out as before, but concentrate more on applying it evenly, rather than on laying down an ample amount.

This is also the coat that shows the self-leveling property of polyurethane to its best advantage. Self-leveling means that if you burst a tiny bubble, or remove something small that may have fallen into the finish, the liquid will move into that "hole" over a few minutes' time and become "level" again. You need to know this now, because you *must not overbrush*. Overbrushing destroys the self-leveling property. You should put it on, even it out quickly, then step back and let the polyurethane do its job.

When you're done, seal up the open cans, dispose of the poly brushes and paper towels, and get out of that room. Any movements in there will kick up dust. Remember, we hate dust. Limit all activity in the room if possible for the half-hour it takes to get a "skin" over the top of the finish. After that, you can safely move the item as long as you don't touch the polyurethane.

Figure 6-24. Cover well with water before sanding.

Figure 6-25. A gentle touch is needed with #400 sandpaper and water.

Final Buffing—For Satin Finish Only

Most of the time you can safely handle your furniture after 24 hours. But keep in mind that the polyurethane will not reach its ultimate hardness for many days. Treat the piece gently for awhile.

I like to wait about 48 hours after I've applied polyurethane before I go back over it to remove any slight dust-caused roughness from the finish. The first technique is the paper bag trick.

Take a brown paper bag, the kind you get at the supermarket, and cut out a piece about the size of your hand. Using this paper as you would sandpaper, gently rub along the direction of the grain. If you see any tiny scratches from the paper you know that you must wait at least another day for this technique. If not, continue to buff the finish gently until you feel no more tiny specks in the finish.

If the roughness is too deep in the finish for the paper bag trick to work, you will have to sand again with #400 or #600 wet/dry sandpaper and use another coat of polyurethane.

Figure 6-26. A paper bag works wonders for a smooth finish.

Figure 6-27.

ALL ABOUT SPRAYING POLYURETHANE— ESPECIALLY FOR GLOSS LOVERS

Polyurethane in a spray can has been around for many years but has never really caught on. The idea was great—especially if you wanted a flawless gloss finish. Just lay on an ample coat with a brush, sand it perfectly smooth, then finish up with a perfect spray coat from an aerosol can.

Too bad it never worked that way. The trouble was that no spray can had a spray nozzle worth a darn. Not only was it nearly impossible to spray without runs, but the cans had a nasty habit of spitting out tiny bits of solids that made little potholes in the finish. But now, surprise! At least two companies I know of have redesigned their sprayers to eliminate the problems.

Figure 6-28. Flecto and McCloskey have come out with adjustable direction sprayers that have an oval-shaped spray pattern that provides excellent results without the old problems.

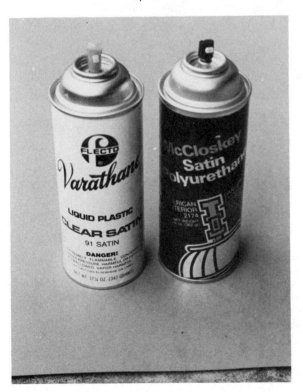

Older-style sprayers concentrated the spray into a small pattern that almost guaranteed runs. Flecto and McCloskey solved the problem by designing an oval spray pattern that allows for a more uniform spray—without heavy concentration in the center of the pattern.

Spraying Techniques

The most important instruction for spraying, as with staining, is to work level. Let gravity work for you. Do the top first. When that's dry enough, usually in ten minutes, turn the piece onto its side and do the other side. While the new oval-shaped spray pattern is a tremendous advancement, it's still possible to hold the can too close while you're spraying a vertical surface and cause a run.

Hold the can about a foot from the surface and move it so that you're pointing the can away from the piece. Start spraying with a sweeping motion as you cover the piece. Continue the motion beyond the edge of the piece, then come back again from the other direction. Just make sure you keep the can at a constant 12 inches or so from the surface.

After you cover the surface one time, turn the piece to the next surface (a 90-degree turn is required) and cover it with another light coat from that direction.

Your banning of dust is still required, but the spray dries to the dust-free point in about five minutes—much faster than the brush-on variety.

Don't Get Greedy

Resist the urge to get every last drop of spray from the can. Every aerosol has some impurities just itching to wreck your finish, and those little gremlins like to hide on the bottom of the can. So if you get to the point where you want to shake the can to see if there's any more in it, you're pushing your luck. Be a big spender and open a fresh can.

Whether or not you want to go beyond two coats of polyurethane is up to you. No

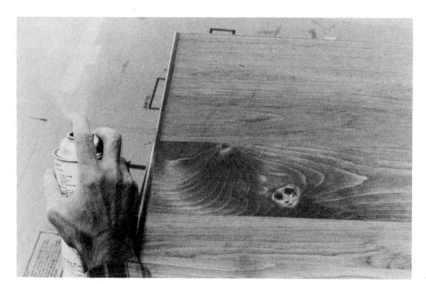

Figure 6-29 a., b., and c. Start and finish off the piece, staying 12 inches from the surface.

a

b

c

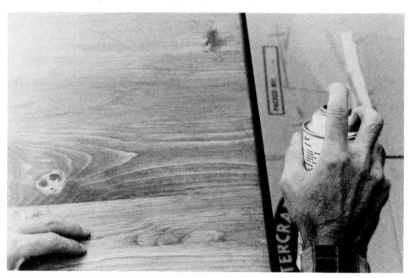

need to get paranoid about alcohol or water affecting your furniture. Two coats are plenty unless you have a bar in your living room and live below the high tide mark.

I will say this, though: I was proudly shown a pine paymaster desk that my customer had finished with eleven coats of gloss polyurethane. It was one of the most magnificent pieces of furniture I had ever seen. I would have bet anything that it was made of glass.

If you've read this far it's obvious that you'd consider doing even more to achieve the finest finish possible. If so, I'm proud of you. This next step requires very little expense; just another sheet of #600 wet/dry sandpaper and some soapy water.

Simply wet-sand the final coat of polyurethane with the #600 sandpaper and the soapy water, using very little pressure. You want to barely drag the sandpaper along the direction of the grain. The soapy water holds the tiny bits of finish you're sanding in suspension until you wipe it off. Then wipe dry with a paper towel. What you'll achieve with this step will be a perfectly smooth surface.

Items used to finish the Bailey nightstand:

1 sheet #220 sandpaper

1 tack cloth

1 pint "American Maple" Private Blend Stain

½ pint "Satin" Private Blend Polyurethane

1 sheet #400 wet/dry sandpaper

1 sheet #600 wet/dry sandpaper

1 can Flecto "Satin" Aerosol Spray

a 1" poly brush

a 3" poly brush

1 roll paper towels

STENCILING

While traditional wood stain with a clear polyurethane finish coat continues to be the overwhelming choice of do-it-yourselfers—nearly 95 percent—there has been an increasing trend toward decorating ready-to-finish furniture with

Figure 6-30. The finished Bailey nightstand. A $59 chest in $150 clothing.

painted designs. Stenciling is the art of applying these designs by painting through a cut-out design.

Stenciling has been used by nearly every culture since the beginning of recorded history, so we're not talking about some new fad. What we are talking about, however, is the certainty that anyone with minimal artistic ability (that's me) can create a unique piece of furniture rather easily. This is mainly due to the availability of new materials, namely pre-cut stencils and easy-to-use acrylic paints.

Nearly a dozen pre-cut stencil manufacturers make hundreds of easy-to-use patterns and provide specialty paints. Stencil styles range from American Colonial, which is the most popular, to Contemporary. You'll find wide selections of stencils at paint and wallpaper stores, arts and crafts stores, and, increasingly, at ready-to-finish furniture stores. Many of these stores will also have detailed instruction sheets, and in some cases entire books, on creating complex designs with stencils. ,

What You Need

1. *Stencils*—pre-cut, made of either paper or plastic. Some have a self-stick adhesive back; some are the tape-down kind. Two of the major brand names are Stencil Magic and Country Colors.
2. *Stencil brush*—you can even use a poly brush.
3. *Paint*—many stencil makers have their own acrylic paint brands specifically for stencil work. Acrylics work well because they're consistently creamy for easy use and they're water-soluble until dry for easy cleanup. Latex paint will also work well.

4. *Paper plate*—for holding paint.
5. *Paper towels*—for cleanup.
6. *Water.*
7. *Masking tape*—to hold stencil firm while painting.
8. *Soft chalk*—for outlining and positioning the design.

Special Note: The following instructions are general in nature and should be modified by the instructions packed with the stencils you buy if they differ. In other words, I won't be holding the bag if anything goes wrong.

Step 1—Apply Stencil

After staining (if you are staining the piece), but before final finishing, decide exactly where you want your design and make a "test." Outline the design lightly with a piece of soft chalk. Often, just a few marks are enough. Then remove the stencil and inspect. This is to make sure you have the pattern in precisely the right place before you start painting. If it's po-

Figure 6-31.

sitioned correctly, re-tape the stencil down and carefully remove the chalk.

Step 2—Apply Paint

Squeeze paint onto paper plate. Dip the tip of the brush into the paint, then dab the brush up and down on the paper plate vigorously to distribute the paint evenly on the brush (Figure 6-32). You want to work with a *dry brush*, that is, a brush without a lot of paint on it. This prevents any excess paint from seeping under the stencil, causing a sloppy design. It's far safer to use several light dabbings than one heavy coat.

Hold the brush perpendicular to the stencil as shown. Apply the paint through the stencil by using an up and down stabbing motion. If the size of the design permits, work from the outside of the design toward the middle. When all of the openings have been covered by paint, untape the stencil and remove by lifting the stencil *straight up* so that the paint does not smear (Figure 6-33).

That's all there is to it! If you are combin-

Figure 6-33.

Figure 6-32.

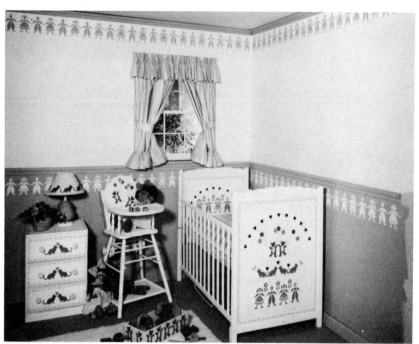

(Photo courtesy of Stencil Magic.)

Figure 6-34. Even the inexpensive pine chest in this baby's room becomes a priceless design original with a little imagination and under ten dollars in stencil costs.

ing designs by overlapping two or more stencils, you must wait until each application dries.

To protect your painted design on furniture, you'll want to apply several coats of a clear finish such as polyurethane. Wait at least 24 hours after your paint is dry and apply with the same techniques described earlier in this chapter.

VICTORIAN COLLECTION

VICTORIAN COLLECTION

VICTORIAN COLLECTION

2054 YESTERDAY'S LADIES

VICTORIAN COLLECTION

2051 ROSE GARDEN BOUQUET

2053 GIFT OF SPRING • BORDERS

2052 FLIGHTS OF FANCY
LADY SLIPPER

COUNTRY COLLECTION

COUNTRY COLLECTION

COUNTRY COLLECTION

2062 BASKET IN BLOOM
BASKET IN BLOOM • BORDER

2063 PRIMITIVE PETS
LEFT AND RIGHT IMAGES

2061 SCHOOL DAYS

FOLK ART COLLECTION

FOLK ART COLLECTION

FOLK ART COLLECTION

2072 LADY BIRDS
LADY BIRDS • BORDER

2071 FEATHERED FRIENDS

2073 IN THE SPARROW TREE

2086
Holiday Merriment

Figure 6-35 a. Here are a few of the hundreds of designs readily available now.   *(Designs courtesy of Country Colors and Stencil Magic.)*

Figure 6-35 b.

Figure 6-36. There are very few wood surfaces
that cannot be dressed up with inexpensive stencil
treatments.

INDEX

PRODUCT INFORMATION REQUEST FORM

Manufacturer: _____

Sirs,

I saw your furniture featured in THE COMPLETE BOOK OF READY-TO-FINISH FURNI-

TURE by Lou Oates. I would like additional information on the following items:

_____

_____

_____

_____

_____

Please list the retail stores in my area where I can place an order:

_____

_____

_____

Please send me your catalog: _____ yes _____ no

Please send information requested above to:

My name _____

Address _____

City _____ State _____ Zip _____

PRODUCT INFORMATION REQUEST FORM

Manufacturer: _____

Sirs,

I saw your furniture featured in THE COMPLETE BOOK OF READY-TO-FINISH FURNI-

TURE by Lou Oates. I would like additional information on the following items:

_____

_____

_____

_____

_____

Please list the retail stores in my area where I can place an order:

_____

_____

_____

Please send me your catalog: _____ yes _____ no

Please send information requested above to:

My name _____

Address _____

City _____ State _____ Zip _____

PRODUCT INFORMATION REQUEST FORM

Manufacturer: _____

Sirs,

I saw your furniture featured in THE COMPLETE BOOK OF READY-TO-FINISH FURNI-

TURE by Lou Oates. I would like additional information on the following items:

_____

_____

_____

_____

_____

Please list the retail stores in my area where I can place an order:

_____

_____

_____

Please send me your catalog: _____ yes _____ no

Please send information requested above to:

My name _____

Address _____

City _____ State _____ Zip _____